BIG CARP

BIG CARP

Edited by Bob Church
Contributors: Chris Ball, Tony Gibson, Graham Kent and Des Taylor

The Crowood Press

First published in 2007 by
The Crowood Press Ltd
Ramsbury, Marlborough
Wiltshire SN8 2HR

www.crowood.com

British Library Cataloguing-in-Publication Data
A catalogue record for this book is available from the British
Library.

ISBN 978 1 86126 911 9

Typeset by Jean Cussons Typesetting, Diss, Norfolk

Printed and bound in Singapore by Craft Print International Ltd

Contents

Kevin Clifford with a very rare Yorkshire Derwent River carp.

Foreword

by Kevin Clifford

Bob Church and The Crowood Press are responsible for putting together a series of successful books about big fish and we have already seen published *Big Tench, Big Barbel* and *Big Pike,* to widespread acclaim and excellent reviews.

This fourth book in the series follows a similar format but deals with big carp. Carp fishing is, of course, a huge and diverse subject, and the source of many of the modern innovations in fishing. It is also hugely popular, probably having more active participants than all the other single species specialists put together. Furthermore, simply because of the substantial revenue generated from carp fishing, a vast array of tackle has been developed and its army of participants has a constant thirst for innovation and knowledge.

Bob Church, both as a hugely successful angler and tackle manufacturer, is ideally placed to observe and understand the modern carp fishing scene. His personal achievements within carp fishing are also not insignificant.

So Bob has wisely chosen a diverse, unusual and interesting mix of contributors this time. They are all well known and respected as expert anglers. They are Chris Ball, who encapsulates the long and respected history of carp fishing, Tony Gibson, who deals with the important aspect of tactics, Graham Kent, who looks at problems involved in tackling a difficult Suffolk carp water and finally, the outspoken Des Taylor, who writes about 'carp fishing my way'.

Undoubtedly this book will be acknowledged as a fitting and welcome addition to the series and as a marvellous addition to carp fishing's rich heritage of literature.

Dedication

I dedicate this book to Dave Steuart, now long retired and living in a lovely house on the banks of the River Test. I certainly learnt so much from Dave in those early days. We became good friends in the early 1960s and exchanged a few fishing tips. His wife Kay was also an excellent fisher and both were all-rounders.

Dave was in on the carp scene at the beginning well before Dick Walker caught the 44lb common that started it all. Dave wrote a book called *Carp: How to Catch Them*, published by Herbert Jenkins (1955). He was catching lots of good double-figure carp up to 15lb 3oz at a time when few were being caught. Dave (now 77 years old) enjoyed the first three books in this series: I hope he thinks the same about this one. One thing is for sure: he helped the carp fishing scene get started – and just look at it today.

Acknowledgements

First, thanks to my chosen four contributors for their good work, Des Taylor, Chris Ball, Tony Gibson and Graham Kent. Also thanks to Kevin Clifford for his foreword. I would also like to thank Ron Randall for his humour and competitiveness during our regular carp fishing sessions, and my daughter-in-law, Kay Church, for typing my final chapter. As always, it's been a good partnership working with my publishers, The Crowood Press. Thanks again to Julie for another fine poem, and to *Coarse Fishing Today* magazine for publishing my regular features, including several on carp.

Finally, thanks to Gavin Walding for his lovely dawn background picture on the cover of this book.

The Carp and the Angler

Julie Emerson

Mirror carp, mirror carp in the pool
Who is the fairest of them all?
Maybe the Crucian with her stealth and style,
Or the common carp teasing the bait for a while.

Cruising around the reeds for food,
Taking the boilie if she's in the mood.
Having fed for days on the fisherman's treats,
One more mouthful and she may be beat…

Thrashing and splashing and fighting with fear,
The rod is bent over, the reel in top gear,
Embracing her beauty as she glides over the net,
This is the one the angler will not forget.

Out to the scales to weigh with pride,
The angler's delight cannot be denied,
Photographs taken to cherish her charm
And back to the water without any harm.

The preparation needed to capture this prize,
Is not always measured purely by size.
Hours on end spent baiting and waiting…
Watching the rod and anticipating…

The art of catching such a wonderful fish,
Is pure determination, stealth and a wish,
Time to reflect and freedom to wait
For the fish of a lifetime to take the bait.

About the Authors

by Bob Church

I found that for *Big Carp*, the fourth book in our big fish series, it was more difficult to get the right balance than with the previous titles. Yet carp are probably the most important species because more anglers are fishing for them than all the other species put together.

So take one very strong personality, who writes a page in *Angling Times* every week – I refer to Des Taylor, of course – and you have a good starting point. Des will be covering carp fishing his way, which I know is much different from the out-and-out carp anglers who just go after very big or record fish. Des is like me in a way, a real all-rounder, but he had done a lot with carp and his chapter is entertaining, controversial and educating.

Now we move on to Tony Gibson, a very good specimen angler and past winner of the Drennan Cup run in *Angling Times* for the best coarse fish of the week, month and finally year. He is a leading member of the Northampton Specimen Group, and as you know they breed very good big fish anglers. His approach to carp fishing has been more than successful over the years. He passes on much of what he has learned while carp fishing, covering tackle, waters, bait, rigs and so on.

Graham Kent may not be a household name in fishing, but he just loves tackling very difficult waters. He lives in Suffolk but is prepared to travel for his fishing. He will tell you about some big fish he has caught, sometimes when there are very few in the lake. Some of his tactics are very good and not widely known. Never one to seek publicity, but with lots of big thirties and over-forties already to his credit, I am sure I have discovered a new star carp fisherman.

Chris Ball is a top carp man and author, who has already been co-author of the best-selling *Century of Carp Fishing* and *King Carp Waters*. It is always good to learn all the background of any sport one is keen on, and Chris knows all there is to know about carp history, from pre-Dick Walker right up to today. Of course, he is also a very good carp angler, so enjoy his chapter.

The foreword to the book has been written by Kevin Clifford, who has been around the carp scene since Dick Walker's heyday. He is general editor-in-chief of *Coarse Angling Today*, *Carp Talk*, and *Pike and Predator* magazines.

1. At Last I Go for Carp

by Bob Church

This is my diary of events as my carp fishing got better with the experience of four seasons of serious fishing for them.

If this had been six years ago I could not have written this opening chapter with any expertise. In my early, very keen specimen hunting days the only waters close to home that held carp was Billing Aquadrome, where a few big ones were caught. Then there was the more prolific River Nene at Northampton, where there was a good head of much smaller common carp. These fish had stunted growth as they were living at the time in the warm water outflow of Northampton's electricity cooling towers. This was from the late 1950s to about 1964.

It wasn't that difficult to catch a good net of smaller ones, or perhaps a little further downstream you might catch four or five of these long chub-shaped 'wildies' – my best was 11lb. I soon began to get fed

Duncan Kay with carp of 29lb 8oz and 21lb 8oz caught using his special Slyme baits, which were the first commercial high-nutrition baits.

up with catching the same size little fish from the river, and where they were much larger – at Billing Aquadrome – there were not many of them at all. I could not handle blank after blank when there was lots of other very good fishing around me. So I gave up trying to catch the carp and became an all-rounder.

In the years that followed I caught the odd carp up to 17lb, but these were still not of great interest. Then I noticed how carp waters were springing up in big numbers all over the country. This meant the number of anglers fishing exclusively for carp was growing, and at a tremendous rate. As I write, and judging by fishing tackle sales, about 70 per cent of UK anglers are now carp fisherman. To service this market there is a carp-only weekly, *Carp Talk*, and a weekly insert called *UK Carp* in *The Angling Times*. Add to this about eight or nine carp angling monthly magazines and you can see the extent of interest we have in this species.

It was 2002, just into the new century, when I came to the conclusion that I had caught large specimens of all the UK freshwater species except the carp, which of course were now the most popular fish in the country. I just had to catch myself a decent carp. One over 20lb would do to start with.

The water must hold big carp for me to be able to catch one. This is Benson, the massive common, at 51lb 10oz to Paul Tanner at Blue Bell Lakes.

My stepdaughter Donna with a low double taken at dusk on floating crust.

I was lucky enough to sort out some fishing for big carp first at two lakes within easy travelling distance and both had good form books. One had a best fish of 43lb, the other a best of 28lb. I realized that the water had to hold big fish for me to have the chance of catching one. Two other waters I would fish for carp in were an old Cambridgeshire gravel pit, and two lakes in the north Midlands, one with just big carp up to 28lb, the other full of good doubles, commons and mirrors.

I had fished quite well with all the other species, so why not carp? Why I had left it so long is hard to say. I suppose I found the tench at Sywell far more obliging to take my bait. Then there was the chub and pike, even specimen eels from the Grand Union Canal were more likely to be caught. The waters were just not available to catch big carp then, that is, in the 1960s. So I set my stool out at fly fishing; I would have been foolish not to, as we had six major trout reservoirs between ten and forty minutes' drive away from home. I then became quite good at trout fly fishing and it held my main summer interest for many years. Then, at the age of 65, I suddenly woke up to the fact that I had this huge gap in my lifetime's angling CV, and decided to give it a bit of a go.

GETTING STARTED

I had plenty of expert carp fishing pals who could advise me. However, it was Gavin Walding and Steven Curtin who put me on the right track, bait wise and how to use it. How could I fail? I filled two extra spools of my new free spool reels with 15lb breaking strain line and dug out a couple of 11ft 2¼lb test Bob Church carp/pike rods. I was also advised to keep my hook/rigs simple, which I did.

I just had to make my own boilies and pop-ups, which we soon sold to the tackle trade, under the Belly Buster label. The first water to concentrate on was the Cambridgeshire pits in April and May with my fishing mate Gareth Hancock, but the tench had taken a great liking to the wild strawberry isotonic boilies. I had as many as twelve in a single session. Every so often I hooked a common carp, and they were so fast and strong that they took me into the tall reeds, where they had a knack of depositing the hook. So first of all I tried

out the stronger tackle, and I was pleased to say had a reasonable degree of success. I could now instantly apply maximum pressure and keep the carp from getting into those reeds, which were growing in five feet of water.

I started to try different boilies and it seemed these wildies liked the yellow-coloured Burnt Scopex bait best of all. Gareth Hancock and I were getting wildies of 6lb, 7lb and over 8lb. They were lovely sleek fish, but we wanted the 20lb+ jobs that it seemed lots of other anglers were catching up and down the country.

Gareth did in fact lose a good common in the 24lb class a year earlier. He had stalked it, then got it feeding on sweetcorn before hooking it on the bait, with three

A 14lb common from the Cambridgeshire pit.

grains on a No. 10 hook hair-rig. Gareth had to hold on pretty tight as the rushes, reeds and lilies were so thick, but the hook hold slipped to his great disappointment. However, we did realize after this incident that there were some larger fish amongst the smaller wildies that were well worth catching.

I had now stopped fishing the lighter tench tackle, concentrating solely on catching a big carp here. I definitely wanted one over 20lb. When I have switched on my determination button in the past, it has meant a PB on the cards. I was determined to get a big carp without bivvying up because I have so many backaches and joint pains, I did not want to aggravate this situation, but dawn till dusk was OK.

We baited up a new swim, using all sorts of broken boilies and minced corn on a gravel bar, in the shallow adjacent gravel pit that ran out some thirty yards into the sixteen-acre pit. This was early on in the day; we then went and fished elsewhere only to return here as the light faded to twilight. After about ten minutes I had a screaming take on my Spicy Crab Beanies (2) and I was in to a powerful fast fighting fish. Even with the 15lb breaking strain line it was going well. Then, as I played it closer to us, we could see it was a long fish, and there was another of similar size swimming with it. Gareth confidently said, 'You have got your twenty,' and I thought so too, right up to the landing net. It was not to be, but I had caught the most beautiful

Steve Curtin plays a big carp.

The end result, a fine 22lb mirror.

wildie I am ever likely to catch. It weighed 14lb only, but the colours and its length made it a special fish. I was happy, and at least they were getting bigger.

The then national barbel record holder Steve Curtin is a very experienced carp angler, but over the last five seasons he has switched to barbel. We have become good fishing mates during this time so he decided to lend a hand with my carp quest. We spent a day at a big gravel pit near his home, one that holds some very big carp. 'Your tackle is fine.' said Steve, 'just keep it simple and sit back and wait.'

A 22lb fish had been caught at first light by an angler bivvied up and we were fishing by 6am. We both had good-looking swims casting across to an island. Lunch-time arrived without a bite and then we heard a 29lb mirror had been landed right round the opposite side of the pit. We were told a lot of carp were gathering there for spawning so we decided to change our swims and drive round.

The fish were spawning all right as they were crashing about violently across a narrow channel towards another island. Steve gave me the choice of spots but all I had was a line bite, while he kept up his good form by landing a mirror of 22lb 6oz, and a lovely, well-marked young eight-pounder. He generously said at packing-up time that he wished I had caught that 20-pounder. I said, 'Steve, it's better if my big carp does not come too easy, as I will respect it more when I get one.'

A STROKE OF LUCK

Then I had a good stroke of luck. Every season I spend a couple of days trout fishing with Ron Randall. He takes me down south to fish dry fly on the River Test and I return the compliment on a trout reservoir. Ron had been saying for some time, 'You must come and try a carp lake that I fish'. For some reason I had never got round to it, but my new carp interest and quest had changed all that. It is a very old seven-acre landscaped private lake.

So on the day England played Argentina in the World Cup 2002 I was at the lakeside to meet Ron at 5.30am. He had pre-baited one corner of the lake with my new Belly Buster isotonic boilies; these were a mixture of four varieties, as I was using up some that had been damaged in their packages in transit, so there was no set flavour to put on as bait. It was absolutely pouring with rain and in my eagerness to get

started I never put my over-trousers on. I got under the brolly and put out my rods – strawberry boilies on one and the nice-smelling Burnt Scopex on the other. The first two hours brought me two jolting line bites, as the rods nearly pulled off their rests.

Then I reeled in the strawberry rod and put on my then new pineapple-flavoured fluorescent pink pop-ups. This I set to fish three inches off the bottom. I cast out to the same spot, wound down to my lead, set the free spool bait runner and before I could sit down it was away with a confident run.

I knew it was a big fish as soon as I struck the hook home as at first it was slow-moving but very, very heavy. I took my time and gradually played the big fish

Not only did I break the 20lb barrier but the 30lb as well, with this lovely old English common of 31lb…

…Followed shortly after by this equally impressive, but not as fat, 28½lb fish.

across the neck of the lake. In the dark water I got a glimpse of the fish and could see it was a big common. Ron was on hand to net it, and at 31lb it was a new lake record. I was completely soaked because of the weighing, photography, and so on, but I was happy.

I couldn't wait to cast out again, so I stayed wet. I was soon in for another surprise, which was to give me a red letter day I would not forget in a hurry. This time, an hour later, it was the Burnt Scopex bottom bait rod that went, again with a good long fight before landing a longer and leaner common carp. It turned the scales at 28½lb and I was one happy angler. Not only had I broken the 20lb barrier, but the 30lb as well.

We stopped fishing at noon, I changed my clothing and generally dried out. A fine lunch and a glass or two of wine, then we watched England beat Argentina on the television. This was doing things in style, I thought, wondering if we would catch any more fish in the afternoon session. As it happened we did, Ron with a wildie of 9lb, while I had another nice wildie of 12lb. At 6pm we packed up and it was still raining. I think I had actually arrived as a proper carp fisherman – three fish for over 70lb, not a bad day's sport in anyone's book. Interestingly, the seven-acre lake had risen six inches during the course of the day, such was the continuous downpour. The feeder stream was now running very coloured and bank high, so I had been lucky.

THE 2003 SEASON

The following summer I again set my stool out to catch a few big carp as I had the year before. My mates were catching monsters –

Spike Harrison had mirrors of 36lb and 30½lb, while Chris Berry caught some beauties in the River Thames up to 38lb. Then Ron broke the fishery record with a lovely common of 32lb 6oz at another lake I fish.

Forty-Pound Monster

I actually went to another water, a very mature fenland gravel pit, with carp in mind and I was in for a bit of a surprise. One of the club members, Stuart Whybrow, told me he had spotted a very big common with three others cruising about probably in preparation for spawning. He said the biggest had to be at least 40lb. When I eventually found these fish I watched them for some time from my concealed position checking out their behaviour pattern.

I put out about twenty Belly Buster spicy crab floaters; these are claret in colour and similar in size and texture to chum mixer. I just wanted to see what would happen. I realized the carp were circling a small bay of the 25-acre lake, keeping to a strict formation. The smallest fish, that was about

Leanne Jayne, an expert carp angler, with a superb 46lb 4oz fish.

14lb, was always in the lead of the group, while second in line was a fish of about 18lb, the third fish looked about 24lb and bringing up the cautious rear was the giant common, which Stuart was right was every bit of 40lb and more. They were all four commons. I watched them for two hours feeding them steadily and gaining confidence. They kept more or less to the same route. The 14-pounder was now mopping up plenty of these free offerings and the next larger fish occasionally sipped the odd floater in.

Eventually I decided I would have to try and catch one. I was no more than two rod lengths away from the group when they passed by, making it all very exciting.

I cast out two cubes of the Belly Buster floating bait on a size 4 strong carp hook. This allowed me a little extra weight to cast the free lined offering on my 15lb nylon line. I soon realized they were prepared to take single baits but were completely ignoring my double hook bait. By the time they came around again I had changed up, threading on a smaller controller in the form of a transparent bubble float half filled with water. The bait now was a single floater.

There was a little cluster of about five free offerings, and the leading 14-pounder took one but kept going. The 18-pounder didn't pick up anything this time and the 24-pounder took a free offering two inches away from my hook bait. But the monster came up at the rear as usual and took its first floater, which happened to be my baited hook.

What happened next has played on my mind many times. On such sturdy tackle I had never experienced such power from any other coarse fish. The carp simply

A lovely winter carp of 23lb 8oz, an opportunist fish.

took over and in a flash it was across to the corner of a little bay that was connected to the main 25-acre lake by a two-foot-deep heavily reed-laced channel. Obviously the fish came into it from the big lake at spawning or pre-spawning time, after which they went back in the main deeper lake.

It ran so fast I had a fairly tight clutch and I always rely on back wind as well. In the past, and since this incident, I had always found this a great method for playing a big fish. On this day the reel handle was ripped from my hands' normal grip – rapping my knuckles several times, such was its speed. But I was in luck – the huge common had charged into some shallow water and almost beached itself. Luckily I was back in contact, but suddenly it was off on another charge over which I had virtually no control. Then came that sick feeling of a slack line – but the fish hadn't come off, it was just motoring back towards me at a tremendous speed. It passed me and went another forty yards to the other corner of the bay. Again I got back in contact with the fish and I began to feel I might land him. Then suddenly it charged into the thick marginal reed beds growing in four to five feet of water and the line parted like cotton.

I had landed the 31-pounder and 28½-pounder not too long ago but they were predictable mere pussycats compared to this animal. For what it was worth, I am pretty sure this fish had never been caught before, so uncaught monsters do exist.

In the next four carp trips I put the hook into two moderate twenty-pounders and landed seven other doubles, six wild long commons to 14lb, and a 14lb mirror. I needed my luck to change with the carp.

While pike fishing on a warm winter's day I came to a nice pool where four carp were lying on the bottom in about five feet of water. They seemed to be moving around a little, sucking away at the bottom stones. Forgetting the piking – I am forever an opportunist – I took the spinner off and replaced it with a No. 4 hook. I kept good and quiet but started to flick some floating smart bait on the water, and, sure enough, they got interested. There were four commons up to doubles and a much larger mirror, which had not taken any offerings. I decided to put on a good-sized piece of bread from my lunch bacon butty roll.

Like magic up came the mirror and took the bread so confidently I had him on the bank in ten minutes, a lovely winter fish of 23lb 8oz.

THE 2004 SEASON

Early the following season, in 2004, I was getting a good few doubles on floaters at the Fenland Pit. Gareth Hancock, whom I often fish with there, excelled after dragging a swim and baiting up; he left it for only two hours before his first run, and he hooked a beauty which I duly netted for him, a fine common of 26lb 12oz. This fell to standard boilie hair-rig tactics, all set up on a Baitrunner reel.

As the spring turned into early summer, I was spending more time fishing the other lake again with good friend Ron Randall. Things all began to fall into place as we put in a combined serious bid to catch some of the big fish in the lake. Losing that (40lb-ish) big common carp the previous year had really fired me up to hook another such specimen.

Then, in six hours of heat wave one day, from noon until 6pm, I landed a brace of 20lb+ carp.

I had caught several good doubles since June, both commons and mirrors, which made me all the more determined to catch a bigger fish. Early season floaters worked to some extent but unlike the previous year

My fishing pal Gareth Hancock has had the best so far from the Fenland pit, this lovely 26lb 12oz common.

I was only getting low doubles. Various boilies hair-rigged on a free running stone ledger had been OK, so instead of changing my bait and rigs, I just changed swims. There is a 60yd-wide channel between the bank and an island and it is quite shallow, no more than four feet in depth. There was a natural swim under a big tree, which caused a few casting difficulties, and also make the final landing of any carp have its dangerous moments.

However, I stood there watching the swim for half an hour and it was quite devoid of a single carp. Then a traveller passed through at good speed, just a low double. Then several more carp followed. None of them stopped, they just quickly swam through the clear, shallow water. I realized this was their M1 motorway for cruising round the lake looking for food. Well, I soon worked out a tactic – I would just catapult out a few boilies and halibut pellets and see if the next lot stopped and fed on them.

It was a dream situation. The first carp literally put the brakes on as he came cruising through the channel, his head went down and his tail waved in the sunlight as he foraged the bottom silt for my free offerings. Soon there were four fish over and around the bait stirring up all the silt in clouds.

Using simple ambush tactics, I just cast out my new Carp Catcher rod equipped with 14lb breaking strain nylon on the reel. My end rig was 15lb brown Mantis braid; I removed the nylon coating for about 6in before tying on a No. 8 hook and a No. 8 swivel at the other end. The overall length of rig is 12–15in. A smallish Stonze weight set up as a simply running ledger was cast out amongst the stirred-up silt area. I didn't have to wait very long as the fish ran off fast with my Belly Buster 'The Mill' Caramel semi-soft 12mm boilie.

This was a good fish making powerful runs into the deeper water, but I got her in the end, a very fat mirror of 25lb 4oz. It

This 25¼lb mirror lost a couple of scales – I suppose when spawning – but it put up a great fight.

had a few spawning scars on its flank but no infections. I treated these with Orabase (for mouth ulcers), which seems to work well on barbel or chub with any sores or scale loss.

I fed the swim up again via catapult with about twenty boilies and five good pouches full of B C halibut pellets. I then made a fresh cast without having to put a new boilie on, as it was still perfectly intact. From my peep hole behind the fat trunk of the tree, I could clearly see more carp coming into the swim. Within ten minutes there was another screaming run and I was into a lovely old English common carp that turned the scales at 22¼lb.

For the third time in six months I had two twenties in successive casts, albeit the other two were pike. That is one sporting hat trick I am very proud of. I then caught further mirrors of 15¼lb and 7½lb. This

totalled 81lb 2oz – not bad for a casual afternoon's fishing during a heat wave. There is no doubt whatsoever that the cruising carp were on the look-out for food. There is also no doubt that carp appear to have a fatal urge to eat as many halibut pellets as you put in front of them. They only leave the spot when it's all gone. I am beginning to enjoy this carp fishing because it's not like it used to be all those years ago, when you had to wait ages for a run. There is far more action for today's carp fisher and I must say I like it better.

I cannot help but observe how many and how big the carp are getting in my local river, the Nene. Two Northampton Specimen Group members have fished for these carp on and off for some years, and Gavin Walding has caught them up to 31½lb just around the Northampton area.

This 22¼lb common gave me a brace of 20lb+ fish in a day. I was on the right track finishing with 88lb 2oz – the halibut pellets were working.

Now Eric Kyte has explored the river downstream these past few summers with some excellent results – nine fish over 20lb and one beauty of 30lb 6oz. Eric's tactics are simple, so he says. First, find the location, that is, observe where a few carp hang out. Second, feed them up for a couple of days. Third, just fish and you will catch them. Eric has similar results on the Great Ouse with corn and luncheon meat. When he fishes for barbel here he has always got carp on his mind also. Taking advantage of one such occasion last season he landed three over 20lb in one day, with the best at 25½lb. So my tip here is watch out what is happening with carp on your local river or canal.

I have tried an all-night session and it produced one lovely common of 14½lb in late May. It wasn't until August that I hit the sort of fish I was after again when I caught a 29lb 2oz old English common

RIGHT: Gavin Walding is a great young carp angler; here he is with the River Nene record fish of 31lb 6oz at the Northampton end of the upper river.

BELOW: Lower down the productive River Nene Eric Kyte caught this wild-looking mirror of 30lb 6oz. The Nene has become one big carp swim.

This 29lb 2oz old common was caught in hot sunshine at midday. This is what I had been hoping for.

Ron's best of the season so far was this hard-fighting mirror of 31lb 2oz.

carp, my season's best. It was a different-looking dark bronze specimen that fought like a demon. On the same day Ron had his best fish of the season too, a finely proportioned mirror of 32lb 2oz.

Ron and I certainly caught well with plenty of carp all summer and we began to get better at catching them. We found our bait was best if we used Nubbies or 'The Mill', a caramel-flavoured barbel or carp semi-soft boilie both from the Belly Buster range.

CONCENTRATING ON CARP – 2005

So we come to the 2005 season, when, instead of trying to do everything and

achieve very little, I concentrated on carp from April to the end of September. Along with Gareth and Ron, my pike-fishing pal Mike Green joined in, but mostly fished on two different lakes.

As mentioned earlier, young top carp man Gavin Walding told me to get out regularly in the daytime when fishing for carp from the beginning of April, and I am so glad I followed his advice. Spring had arrived with persistent very cold easterly winds. If the tackle dealers' moans were anything to go by, not many of us were going fishing until the beginning of May. If you don't try you will never know how it is fishing. I can tell you now Gavin was spot-on. During that colder than normal period I took my best haul of carp and two best individual specimens, I mean I just don't

Gavin Walding's advice proved spot-on when he recommended going regularly from the beginning of April, when carp really start feeding well in the daytime.

Northants Lake: fishing and baiting the same swim in the carp's cruising area at seventy yards close to an island.

normally catch carp of thirty to forty pounds, but I do now.

Being very senior and mixing with some great young anglers in the Northampton Specimen Group does give me an edge. Between them, they catch so many large fish of all species their keenness rubs off on me. I believe you can work things out better when you get older, and plot the downfall of more big fish.

Gavin's tip-off was to make an early start even though it was still cold, with water temperatures around 50°F. The four trips I put in for April were fantastic, I was now making all the right decisions. So in the first ten days of April I fished the same lake and same swim, baiting it up precisely and casting out exactly in the cruising taking spots.

Day 1: water temperature 51°F, bait fluorescent pink pop-up 16mm, fished on short 3in link to swan shot anchor. I thought it was a good start because I didn't expect too much, but I finished with commons of 22lb and 14lb, and an 8lb mirror.

Day 2: water temperature dropped to 49°F and I had only one fish at 21¼lb, an Italian-type mirror, to a Belly Buster Scopex boilie.

Day 3: my best one-session catch. Water temperatures were still low at 49°F, but I landed five carp for 104lb 4oz, which included a new personal best of a 35½lb mirror, almost a leather. It took a 'The

RIGHT: *At 22lb, this well-conditioned common was a good start to the season.*

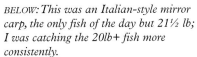

BELOW: *This was an Italian-style mirror carp, the only fish of the day but 21½ lb; I was catching the 20lb+ fish more consistently.*

I was very pleased with this new personal best, an almost leather carp of 35lb 8oz, part of a catch of five fish totalling 104lb 4oz.

Mill' Belly Buster boilie, it put up a great fight and of course I had upgraded my rods to 12-foot Carp Catcher rods, which our firm sells to the trade. At 2½lb test they do the job well. I use 15lb Krystonite for all my specimen fishing these days and of course free for spool reels. I favour the single handle models – why do you want a double handle?

I then had a beauty, a ghost common of 23¼lb on the same bait, a 21½lb common on an orange pop-up, a 14½lb common again on the same caramel Belly Buster and finally a 9½lb common on the orange pop-up. To say I was thrilled would be an understatement. Ron was also catching plenty of fish, but it seemed I had the luck getting the bigger ones.

Day 4: a show-stopper for me. It was 24 April and it had now warmed up, but between us we only had one run, which went to my rod. The session for me began

Bob returns the 23lb 4oz ghost common straight after weighing and a photograph.

at 10.30am, and the one run came at 2pm, when the water temperature had risen five degrees in six hours.

I had put out a very good cast, which dropped under the arch of an overhanging tree of the island. This put my bait in a new position further down the island bank I had previously been fishing. I had changed from the very successful stumpy short-rig for this rod, instead putting on an 18in 15lb Krystonite rig to a swivel one end and a No. 8 hair-rig system for the boilie bait, which was 'The Mill' caramel covered in the same paste. So the bait was right and its position looked very good – as Del Boy would say 'perfick!' I just knew I would get a fish.

My bait had been out for just three minutes when the buzzer screamed, I was into a solid object that was not moving much at all. After five minutes of this and with the fish about seventy-five yards away my line suddenly went slack. I called to Ron, 'It's off,' and quickly wound in thirty yards of line. But no, he was still there! The fish had swum towards me at great speed, giving me the feeling of having come off. Anyway, I was back into the fight and it was a good one. I took a leaf out of my salmon fishing memories of playing big fish. I walked slowly backwards regaining line as I walked forwards to the lake's edge again.

Slowly I brought the big fish to within ten yards of the bank as Ron waited with the largest landing net. The fish came on top briefly and showed itself before taking off on a powerful high-speed run. Fortunately, I was ready for this and I was using back wind as well as a fairly stiff clutch that would give line in an emergency without breaking. After about fifteen minutes Ron netted the massive fat mirror carp. I could hardly believe my eyes. Having caught a 35½lb-pounder the week before, I hadn't expected to catch one that dwarfed it. Ron and Richard weighed and witnessed the fish as I stood by and trembled. It weighed 40lb 7oz. The adrenaline shot put the aches and pains of my back problems out of my mind for a while. To say I was a happy angler at that moment wouldn't even begin to describe it.

The biggest and heaviest so far for me is this well-proportioned 40lb 7oz mirror carp. It gave me some anxious moments in the fight.

Northern Lakes

Mike Green invited Ron and me to his friend's north country carp lakes for a 24-hour overnight session. One lake has carp in to about twenty pounds but plenty of high doubles, and the other is mostly twenty-pounders. There is an added real luxury at each lake by way of fully fitted anglers' cabins.

Mike, who had visited there many times, did the gentlemanly thing and cooked a superb fillet steak dinner and I believe the

champagne count was seven bottles. We baited up with various free offerings but concentrated on Belly Busters Nubbies, which are really a sweet corn mix shaped like a peanut in the shell. I also tried the Colossal Corn that Mike has scored so brilliantly with, using the orange pine-apple and the red savoury. As evening approached Ron had the first run on the Nubbie and was soon netting the one and only koi in the lake, which was last caught at 8lb two years ago. Ron quickly weighed it at 11lb.

Ron caught the one and only koi carp in the lake at 11lb; it had not been caught for two years when it weighed 8lb.

I sprayed my rods out at different angles and to cover all possible cruising paths the carp might move into after dark. We only had one single bleep all night after casting out for the last time with fresh bait at midnight.

Come the dawn I decided to go looking. So I reeled in one rod and left the other, which was in a very good long-range position for Ron to have. I found one clear bubble float in the bottom of my bag, half-filled it with a little water, put on a No. 2 hook and pinched half a loaf of bread from the hut.

I scattered a few free offerings of floating bread at the bottom of the wind end of the lake. Two were taken no more than three yards from the bank. So out went my floating bread and I was soon into a lovely common carp of 17½lb. While playing it Mike

arrived to tell me all floating baits were banned. It was too late to do much about it so I enjoyed the moment.

Mike then asked me to go and fish the other lake, where they really take the corn (Colossal) well. In an hour and a half I had two nice double-figure mirrors using Mike's tackle and red Colossal corn bait, their weights being 15½lb and 14½lb.

Ron phoned through on the mobile to say he wanted to leave at noon so would I make my way back to our hut. As I was about 150 yards from the hut I heard the sound of a long run from one of Ron's buzzers. He was quickly into the fish, a mirror, which at 20¼lb, was the best of the pleasant 'old boys' ' outing; the rod was the one I cast out at midnight 12 hours earlier, so the old Nubbie Belly Buster came good in the end for Ron.

Came the dawn and I went stalking with floating bread crust; this 17lb 8oz common could not resist it.

Ron's last-minute 20lb 4oz mirror carp from the lake in the north.

At 32lb 8oz, this was my personal best for a common carp. I was so pleased to end my personal carp season on such a high note.

The End of the Season

So we came to the end of September 2005, when I suggested to Ron that we should have a final go at the carp just to see if we could go out on a high. He agreed we should do Saturday so it would only be a morning for me as Northampton Town were playing at home in the afternoon.

Once more I carried out my baiting up approach but I cast the rods out first. One landed perfectly about a couple of feet from a lily patch, which in turn backed on to the island. For bait I hair-rigged two soft boilies I was trying out. Apart from that, I had the usual Stonze set-up on a free-running lead and No. 6 hook with 15lb Krystonite as my reel line and my hook link.

At exactly twelve noon the buzzer screamed to a very fast run. I was into the fish quite quickly, but even so she found the edges of the lilies. I gave this fish a lot of pressure, such is my confidence in the tackle. A great method I have been using and I again did with this fish, is to walk backwards then quickly forwards – this is an old salmon fisher's trick because playing

35

a fish like this seldom lets it get out of control while in the middle of the lake.

When I got the carp close to the bank she started to give me a hell of a fight, equal to the best of the year. She made three powerful runs towards quite a big lily bed to my left, and actually got into the bed twice, but fortunately she came out the way she went in as I applied maximum side strain.

Ron netted her for me and we stared at a magnificent old English common carp of 32½lb, a new lake record. I've had a 31lb common before and Ron has had a 32lb 6oz fish before. I was so happy even the football team drawing at home yet again couldn't pull me down off the high.

That ended my carping towards the end of September. The 32lb 8oz was a PB for a common carp. My grand total for the 2005 six-month period came to twenty-one fish over twenty pounds, with lots of doubles. These came from four different lakes.

It's time to call it a day until next April, when, as I found this year, some of the largest carp in the lake begin to feed in earnest again. Because they have not been active they seem to feed well during the daytime, which suits me fine.

Ron's heaviest carp so far, a 35lb 8oz leather mirror.

The northern lake had the luxury of a fitted-out fishermen's hut.

Spike with this fine grass carp that went almost 30lb; he now thinks he can catch the UK record from a Bedfordshire pit we fish.

Bob caught this yellow leather from the Grand Union Canal at Milton Keynes – canal fishing is excellent!

GOOD TIPS TO TAKE NOTE OF

I found out that carp are on the move quite a lot during daytime and they like to be near some feature – round the margins of an island, or beds of lilies, or some obstacle like a fallen branch of a tree. Once I have located their cruising route I bait up with halibut pellets, 8mm, then fire out some free hookbait samples, starting with about twenty over an area about as big as a normal-sized living room. There will probably be no carp there at this point, but I guarantee there soon will be. Hair-rig one of the same boilies on and you're away. By the way, I swear by 15lb BS Krystonite, I now use it for everything, including pike spinning, salmon leaders, barbel and of course all my carp fishing. It's not let me down at all, and I've caught plenty of bigger than my normal fish this year. As well as its great strength, it knots well and is completely transparent in water. The low-diameter fluoro-carbon-coated polymer also helps, I am sure.

Sometimes I catch these long chub-shaped wild common carp; they fight like fury, as this 20lb 8oz specimen did.

One thing that that has troubled me is that I keep buying all the carp magazines and read about all these fancy rigs, but a straightforward free-running lead or stone is all I've ever used and I haven't missed any.

I now know why the whole country has gone carp crazy, no matter if it's match fishing, pleasure fishing or specimen hunting. I wonder what the late, great Dick Walker would say if he knew what he had

started? As I write, on 1 March 2006, it's very cold, but in a month's time I will be out carping again and try to repeat, if not better, my records. Although I am a confirmed all-rounder, I must admit I've enjoyed this carp fishing as much as any of the best I have had before.

Now have a good read and learn what my four selected expert guests have to say…

2. The Development of Carp Fishing

by Chris Ball

So where do I start to tell of the incredible rise of fishing for carp as a sporting species here in the UK. It's still a rollercoaster of a ride that's running at a rate of knots as I contemplate the thought of writing this chapter in the spring of 2006.

Carp fishing started from the need to eat a plentiful food source throughout Europe and beyond to, hundreds of years later, become the greatest phenomenon to hit UK angling during the latter half of the last century and into the present one. Strange as it may sound, two Beatles' song titles come to mind, *The Long and Winding Road* and *Magical Mystery Tour*; to my mind, both aptly describe what has happened.

Carp were present in Britain as long ago as the late fourteenth or early fifteenth century, and only a little later were being reared here too. At some stage around this time, the use of rod and line as a means of survival – to catch a food source – evolved into becoming 'recreational' and a pleasurable interest to follow. But when it came to carp, well, that was something different. I only have to delve into the written works of Robert Marston, the famous editor of the *Fishing Gazette*, who in 1904 wrote, 'There are exceptions to all rules, but as a rule I should not advise an angler to waste much time in fishing for carp – life is too short and the art of catching carp takes too long to learn.'

Early Pioneers

This statement comes on the back of clear evidence that carp were being introduced for stocking (angling) purposes from the 1890s onwards. Further evidence comes from a vast research programme conducted by my friend and business partner, Kev Clifford, who revealed that a prominent role in the introduction of king carp (selectively bred carp which displayed fast-growing characteristics) into the UK was being masterminded by a gentleman named Thomas Ford, who ran a company called Manor Fisheries. This Caistor, Lincolnshire-based business supplied a good many king carp at the time, which were distributed throughout the length and breadth of the country.

However, I can't progress much further without mentioning an incredible character called Otto Overbeck. Here are some gems from Kev Clifford's book, *A History of Carp Fishing*, published in 1992:

It was the name and deeds of Otto Overbeck that really caught the public's attention and there is no doubt that Overbeck was the master carp angler of his time. He went to considerable lengths in his study of carp, both at Croxby Pond (which had held carp since the early 1800s) and with captive fish confined to a large concrete tank outside his home in Grimsby. He considered and developed various special

Chris Ball carp fishing at a Surrey lake.

baits and refined several aspects of carp fishing. Overbeck was born in 1860 and his association with Croxby's carp began in about 1890. Over the next thirty years he caught many carp, twice landing five in a day, and during this time he acquired some understanding of the biology of the carp and their habits. He was dismissive of a number of fallacies previously held about carp and, through his scientific training and background, was instrumental in bringing about some logical thinking into carp fishing. The acclaim he received at the time as the country's most successful and knowledgeable carp angler was largely deserved.

However, other anglers also started to gain some kind of association with carp, such as Mr J. Goodwin, who fished at long range (using a Malloch Sidecaster reel, a kind of forerunner to the fixed-spool reel) at Richmond Park, London. And on the horizon was a notable carp fishery that was to hold the limelight for many years: Cheshunt Reservoir, which, like Richmond Park, was in the London area (North London in fact).

Extending to over fourteen acres in 1910, it was leased by the long-established and famous Highbury Angling Society. Amongst its members were many influential and well-known anglers/writers of the time, including William Senior, Hugh Sheringham and Robert Marston. When the 1911 season started, a string of big

Croxby Pond pictured in the early 1950s.

A Cheshunt Reservoir cased carp from 1913.

carp were caught by members, the largest weighing a creditable 17lb 2oz. Cheshunt was to rule the roost for the next fifteen years or so, culminating in a new record carp weighing 20lb 3oz, landed by John Andrews in October 1916.

You can get an idea of how big carp could grow in this country at that time by looking at the records of fish that were either netted or found dead. Records show that Virginia Water in Surrey yielded a 26lb fish in 1912, Hampton Court was the scene for a netted 37-pounder in 1916, a 24-pounder was reported from a Birmingham reservoir in 1921, and in 1921 at a Kent lake someone found a 26lb mirror floating dead in the margins.

ALBERT BUCKLEY AND A NEW RECORD

One of the most notable events to happen in carp fishing history was the capture of a new record carp in July 1930 from Mapperley Reservoir, Nottingham – a monster of 26lb. This 29-acre reservoir sits on the Shipley Estate, which dates back to medieval times, and had fourteen farms, its own railway station, water supply, gas works, a canal and wharf! The carp had been stocked into the reservoir around 1911 by the then owner Alfred Miller, and though the actual number of carp released into the water is shrouded in mystery, one thing was for sure – they found the environment to their liking. For many years they lay unnoticed save by a gamekeeper or suchlike, who maybe glimpsed a vast dark shape gilding through the shallow water in the 'inlet pool' at the very head of the reservoir or witnessed a huge fish leaping clear of the water on a early summer's morning.

It wasn't until the early part of the 1930 fishing season that an individual, Albert Buckley, who would leave his mark forever in the annuls of carp fishing history, was to taste success. Having fished a number of the other lakes on the Shipley estate mainly for pike, Albert was told that the reservoir held some monster carp, which no one had ever landed on rod and line. In early July, Albert and colleagues were fishing for roach at the reservoir when a friend fishing close by hooked a fish from the dam wall which he said was a big carp. However, it didn't stay in contact for long and was soon lost. Albert watched as his friend re-tackled and cast in. Sure enough, within a short space of time his float disappeared again and another big carp was hooked. This one went shooting out into the lake at great speed, then stopped and turned back the way it had come, arriving back at the foot of the dam wall in double-quick time. Then in spectacular fashion it shot off parallel along the dam wall for over two hundred yards with angler and friends in hot pursuit! Then it suddenly stopped just a few yards out from the dam wall. Albert peered into the clear water and just perceived the end of its tail. That was the signal for the fish to charge headlong straight up the lake, and after all hundred and fifty yards of line was taken, the line broke, fortunately near the hook. Albert estimated the fish was on for over two and a half hours – what excitement.

Albert Buckley had noted that on this day the wind was blowing from a westerly direction straight towards the dam and that a number of big fish, almost certainly carp, were heard crashing out of the water in the general area. The following Saturday, Albert and friends were back on the dam wall. The wind was still blowing from the west and the carp again fed in the deep water in front of the dam wall. Albert's hapless friend again hooked a number of big fish that day only to lose them all!

On Saturday, 19 July, Albert and his father set forth to do battle with the elusive

Albert Buckley's big carp catch from 1930, the 26-pounder record breaker at the front.

Mapperley carp. The wind was still blowing from the west as the pair set up on the dam wall, Albert's father fishing a hundred yards further down. Albert cast in at the spot where he'd seen his friend hook a number of carp on previous visits. He used honey-flavoured paste fished hard on the bottom with four or five pieces of paste thrown in around his float. Nothing happened for an hour, then Albert saw a great carp roll eighty yards away. After a few more minutes several other carp jumped much closer to the float. Suddenly his float vanished beneath the waves and a great battle began. Having witnessed the disasters to his friend two weeks before, Albert was well equipped with plenty of line on the reel. Even so, it took around 150 yards before the fish stopped and very slowly came back toward him. Exactly 55 minutes later the net wielded by his father lifted around the first verified carp ever taken on rod and line from Mapperley Reservoir. It weighed 16lb. Within ten minutes of arriving back he hooked another and after a similar battle a 14-pounder was banked.

This brace of carp landed on light tackle showed Albert he was on the right track to land more and the following Thursday, 24 July, was set aside for his next visit. Fishing alone that day, Albert shortly afterwards wrote the following, which appeared in *The Angler's News*, a fishing paper of the time:

On July 24th I got four carp, 9lb, 11lb, 15lb and 26lb. I caught them all on with brown bread paste mixed with honey. It took me nearly 1.5 hours to land the 26-pounder. I have a very large landing net but I could not use it, so I had to use the gaff, which broke, so I had to finish up getting him out with my hands. As soon as I got the carp on the bank I conveyed it to the gamekeeper's house nearby. His scales weighed up to 25lb but these would not weight the fish. At this the keeper guessed it to be between 28lb and 30lb.

Albert could not get it properly weighed until 8.30pm when a weight of 26lb was recorded.

This carp above all others inspired numbers of other anglers to try their hand at fishing for carp; indeed, a full account by Buckley appeared in a very influential fishing book by one of the catalysts of modern-day carp fishing, Deny Watkins-Pitchford, better known as the writer and artist 'BB', in his book published at the end of the Second World War, *The Fisherman's Bedside Book*. In the years that followed Buckley's capture the greater availability of carp swimming in UK waters meant numbers of fish up to 10lb in weight were captured, mostly by accident (and a great many were lost, leaving the angler with a racing pulse as they were spectacularly broken up). But evidence now and then showed that there were indeed monster carp swimming unseen in British waters. Mapperley itself provided confirmation of this when at least one fish was found washed up dead after being swept over the slipway at the dam end – rumour suggests some were in the 30–35lb class. In 1937 Mapperley again provided further evidence that it held big carp when Les Brown captured a 23.75lb mirror (and followed that up in 1941 with 20½lb mirror). But at the end of the Second World War another famous water started to stamp its authority on the pursuit of fishing for big carp – Dagenham Lake in Essex.

Essex Rules OK!

The club that was involved in the development of Dagenham Lake, the Beacontree and District Angling Society, was formed in 1932. Barely a dozen miles or so from central London was the society's Boyer's Pit. It was stocked with carp in late 1932 and the following year other carp were placed in the water, then in 1938 a batch of Hungarian carp were added. All the fish, not just the carp, grew in the rich environment. In 1943 a 16¾lb mirror was landed by Harry Evans, which drew attention to the place for this was indeed a big carp landed by fair angling means on rod and line.

Come early July and within two days of one another came two glorious 20-pounders, the first a 22-pounder landed on maggots by Arthur Horwood, the second a deep-bodied 23lb mirror by Frank Scott. Soon speculation was rife that Dagenham had the potential to produce a new record carp, though as a number of dedicated anglers who fished for the Dagenham carp were to find out soon enough, those fish weren't going to be a pushover.

Major George Draper was one such angler. He was keen, often fishing two, sometimes three, nights a week in the pursuit of the carp. He knew he was getting close to landing something special, but had to wait a further year before that golden chance came and a near record carp finally plunged into his waiting net. At 25lb 9oz it was the second largest carp ever seen on the end of a line in the country. Like a number of the large carp caught at the time it was set up and we have details about this mirror – 33½in long by 30in girth. That fish was the last recorded Dagenham carp for 1947.

Richard Walker and his 22¾lb Dagenham carp from July 1952.

The following year, 1948, was a bumper season for Beacontree and District members. Right from the off, double-figure carp were landed, and as June passed into July bigger fish were caught: an 18lb 14oz common was recorded on 5 July, and then another 20lb carp was captured, this time by a name forever associated with the Dagenham carp, Harry Grief. I once met this gentleman at the Carp Society 'Richard Walker Remembrance Conference' in June 1988. Though no doubt slightly overawed by the occasion he appeared onstage with other surviving members of the famed Carp Catchers' Club to give a glimpse of what fishing for carp was really like in the 1940s/1950s. He still talked of carp in an excited voice as he relived some of those Dagenham moments.

George Draper captured his second twenty-pounder a few weeks after Harry's fish and days later the best Dagenham carp of the year was taken by a Len Singer at 21lb 15oz, which displayed nice proportions of 30in length by 27½in girth.

By contrast, 1949 only produced one noteworthy carp from the lake, yet another twenty-pounder, this one falling to the rod of a Mr Stewart at 20lb 2oz.

As if hiding slightly from the limelight for just a moment, Dagenham carp burst forth in ever greater numbers during 1950, with Harry Grief coming within a whisker of beating the Mapperley record fish with a 25¾lb common – it turned out to be the largest recorded from this marvellous fishery, but not Harry's last big 'un from the lake. Nearly fifteen years after catching his first notable carp from the pit, Harry Grief banked a mirror of 23¾lb on the opening day of the 1958 season.

Richard Walker caught his first 20lb carp at Dagenham on the last day of July 1952 along with a 17½lb mirror the same afternoon – it caused much excitement and admiration amongst members.

Though Dagenham reigned supreme as a major carp fishery throughout the late 1940s and early 1950s (during the 1950 season alone the first eight places in the *Angler's News* Notable Fish List for carp, including three 20lb+ fish, came from Dagenham). However, it was about to be eclipsed by another lake far away on the other side of the country. After Redmire Pool was discovered in late 1951, it would cast its vast net over carp fishing for the next forty years and become a dominant force driving carp fishing to new exciting heights that the general angling public could never have dreamed of.

Redmire Pool

I make no apologies for the amount of space that Redmire takes in this chapter for such was its earth-shattering effect on carp fishing in Britain. The unearthing of a small, almost insignificant reach of still-water by anglers who fished in the Ross-on-Wye district of Gloucestershire was to bear much fruit.

Angling in the early 1950s was only just starting to recover from the war years, and not unreasonably most people just wanted to catch anything, let alone a carp, which had a formidable reputation of taking a lifetime to grow big, and if you were ever unlucky enough to find yourself attached to one... well it was goodbye to hook, float and several yards of line.

Yet anglers by nature love stories of big fish and places that hold them and it is this spark that probably first alerted one or two members of the Gloucestershire Anglers' Association to the potential of a small private pond near Llangarron to the west of Ross-on-Wye.

This pool, around three acres in size, had been formed possibly as far back as the early seventeenth-century by damming the small stream that had gouged out a path in a fold of the Gloucestershire countryside. It held trout sometime in the early 1930s, though its main purpose in life was to supply water to the big house on the hill – Bernithan Court. This task was achieved by installing a hydraulic ram pump in a small pumphouse to one end of the dam (this small building still stands today). Continual problems with weed and scum clogging the intake of the pump valve forced the owners to look at ways to improve the situation. Help was sought from the company that had supplied the trout to the Court – The Surrey Trout Farm and United Fisheries.

Many carp anglers will have heard of

carp called 'Leneys', named after the man who headed the Surrey Trout Farm, Donald Leney. It was probably the farm's suggestion that stocking with carp might alleviate the problems with weed and in turn help the pump situation. In any event, carp fishing history is blessed with documentative evidence that Bernithan Court Water (renamed Redmire Pool in late 1952) was stocked with fifty yearling carp on 10 March 1934. They came from the Midland Fishery (part of the Surrey Trout Farm operation) at Nailsworth, some thirty miles or so from Ross-on-Wye. These prime, fast-growing, mainly mirror carp of the Galician race of carp, were released into a water with a haven of food that had little else to feed on it.

The massive consequences of this event were to unfold less than twenty years later, and what happened changed the face of carp fishing forever.

The First Anglers

When researching my book *The King Carp Waters* (Crowood Press 1993) during the late 1980s, I went with Chris Yates to the Royal Arms in Langarron – probably the closest pub to the lake – to meet with a character that Chris and Rod Hutchinson had met in the pub when they first joined Jack Hilton's Redmire syndicate back in 1972. His name was Jack Farmer (Jack the Roadman) and he had known the area around the Bernithan estate since he was a boy. Though he'd been on the land surrounding the pool after the Second World War, he could never remember seeing any big fish floating around, though he did 'snitch' many an eel from the pool.

One of the first accounts of giant carp being spotted in Bernithan Court Water came from Bob Richards, a Gloucester tobacconist; he reported the following in the Carp Catchers' Club letters:

I first heard of it in the autumn of 1950 from a member of the club I joined to get experience on fishing generally and to learn the ways and outlook on fishing from those men who go fishing in inter-club matches etc. The member who told me, Harold Bolton, had fished there all one night and the next day, in the year I believe 1949, quite by chance owing to the River Garron being in flood at the time. He told me he had no luck at all but during the day while fishing from the punt he saw a monster carp cruising about near the surface.

He explained to me it was very weedy and difficult to fish from the banks because of the weed, but I could doubtless get permission if I cared to try, which I did that evening, and had permission to fish the following Thursday; the owner, Mrs Barnardiston, asking me to call at the Court for the paddle for the punt, which on all occasions I did.

Bob Richards managed the odd day in the autumn of 1950, but without luck. However, the first Bernithan carp had been landed a few months before, a six-pounder to a Mr Munro.

With renewed vigour, Bob Richards, determined to come face to face with a big carp, fished a total of ten trips during the 1951–52 season, often accompanied by his friend, John Thorpe. On one of the trips Bob hooked a carp that promptly ran into the weed and broke him. He was shaken by the power of the thing – would he get another chance?

Eric Higgs was the young son of one of the workhands on the estate; he met Bob a few times and was no doubt interested in seeing someone fish at the pool. By early October 1951 Bob Richards had talked to young Higgs with a view to him baiting up an area – breadpaste thrown into a spot out from the big willows that formed such a

Bob Richards fishing from the very spot he caught a new record of 31¼lb in October 1951.

striking feature close to the dam on the west bank.

Bob had planned to go fishing the following week, on the 3 October, the weather being quite mild for the time of year. Little did Bob realize that this day's fishing was to be a turning point from which carp fishing would never look back. He had six bites that day, several fish were lost, but the last one hooked turned out to be a new British record carp in the shape of the country's first carp landed over thirty pounds – a magnificent 31¼lb linear mirror.

Redmire Pool pictured through Richard Walker's camera in the mid-1950s.

Though the fish had perished at capture it eventually turned up at the doorstep of a gentleman named Richard Walker. This man was a passionate angler with real interest in carp – he was probably one of the, if not *the*, most successful carp fisher of the time. Richard made a fine job of mounting the fish and was naturally more than interested to hear more of the water from where it was caught. During the winter of 1951–52 plans were laid for other anglers to fish at Bernithan, including Richard Walker, his friend Pete Thomas and another carp fisherman of note, Dick Kefford. All had arrangements in place as soon as the following season started.

These circumstances opened the floodgates to the captures of large carp hardly anyone at the time could have dreamed of. The first weekend of the season Pete Thomas, fishing with Walker, landed the second largest carp recorded, a mirror of 28lb 10oz. Maurice Ingham from Louth, Lincolnshire banked a 24¾lb mirror in late July, then in September Richard Walker landed what was to become one of the most historic carp this country has ever produced. In the early hours of 13 September 1952 Dick Walker landed, with essential help from his friend Pete Thomas, a carp so large that the angling world at first thought it must be a hoax.

At the time the impact of a carp weighing 44lb landed from a small pool on the Welsh border is hard to imagine. Think of it as similar to someone running a three-minute mile at the next Olympics! The

Dick Walker with his record 44-pounder from Redmire – a truly giant freshwater fish.

difference was as stark and as great as that. Better still was Walker's decision to arrange to have the fish transported to the London Zoo at Regents Park. It became an overnight sensation and over the years masses of anglers and other folk came to look in wonder at this truly monstrous freshwater fish.

With *Angling Times* commencing publication the following year (1953) and Dick Walker writing a weekly column, carp fishing was given much attention. And of course Redmire Pool (renamed by the request of Bernithan's tenant) got plenty of coverage. When Dick Walker landed a 31¾lb common (true weight 34lb, but that's another story) on the opening weekend of the 1954 season, people started to

talk as though he was a new messiah in fishing – and in many ways he was. To hold both first and second place of a species in the freshwater record list was something very few, if anyone, has done before or since (I'll have to think about that one.)

Others fished at Redmire Pool through the 1950s; in the main they were friends of members of the Carp Catchers' Club, (the original specimen group). Indeed, a number of guests landed big carp, including Pat Russell, Jack Opie, Derek Davenport, Bob Rutland, May Berth-Jones (wife of CCC member Gerry) and Harry Kefford (brother of another CCC member, Dick). Maurice Ingham caught another twenty-pounder in 1954 and Bob Richards another 30-pounder in 1956. Fish like these were just not around to be caught in this country at the time, unless of course you fished at Redmire!

Another milestone event in Redmire's history came in the early autumn of 1959, when Gloucester farmer and avid carp fisherman, Eddie Price, banked the UK's second forty-pound carp. This carp went on, twenty-one years later, to become Chris Yates' record mirror of 51½lb.

The Redmire Monsters

This subject would fill a book in itself, but suffice it to say that the stories surrounding *uncaught* monster carp at Redmire almost rival the accounts of fish that *were* caught!

Many moons ago, in 1970, when I was corresponding with Dick Walker he wrote and told me, 'I don't doubt that at one time there were carp in Redmire weighing in the region of 60lb or 70lb. My friends and I often saw fish that I would guess as being in this category, though I don't think there were ever more than two or three of that size in the pool.' Few of the early captures of big carp caught at Redmire were returned to the water to be spotted again – they had either been removed or had died. This meant comparisons with other fish swimming about were plainly out of the question. However, in the early summer of 1954 Richard Walker handled a carp somewhat larger than his record 44lb fish. The following extract

A famous carp fishing picture from nearly fifty years ago – could this be one of the monster uncaught carp from Redmire Pool?

comes from a letter I have from Dick dated 29 July 1970:

The biggest fish that I was ever able to weigh at Redmire was one that I caught in a landing net in 1954. This was a female fish that had been driven into shallow water by two or three smaller male fish, that being the year when the fish decided to spawn towards the end of June.

This very large female fish had been driven so far into shallow water close to the bank that it was lying on its side and looked in some danger of remaining permanently stranded, so I paddled out, clapped my big carp net over it, pulled it to the shore, weighed it and then carried it down, with some effort, to the deep water near the dam and released it. This fish weighed 58lb; but I must add that it was considerably distended with spawn.

Then we have the now famous picture that Eddie Price took in July 1958. This quote comes from Eddie Price's diary written at the time:

On the Sunday, midday, I took the punt out and drifted down the lake to observe any fish basking and to see if there was much fry about. There was little fry but I saw and photographed what was probably the biggest carp I shall ever see. Its head and part of its back protruded from the thick weed masses, and without exaggeration it seemed a foot across its back. I was only a yard from it. On my drifting nearer it slowly drew its bulk from the weed and slid silently from my view into the depths, leaving me with bulging eyes and a memory of a lifetime.

Could the picture opposite depict one of the legendary monster carp seen by umpteen Redmire anglers? We'll never know for sure, and that's the way I'd like it to be left… we all need that childhood dream of monster carp that never get caught.

Death and Rebirth

The early 1960s at Redmire Pool maybe showed that the carp had learned quicker than the anglers, as catches of carp at Redmire over 20lb dwindled – five being caught in three years – before the country become locked in ice for 12 weeks starting around Christmas 1962. The great freeze-up of 1962–63 is little remembered by anglers these days, although at the time it caused havoc at thousands of stillwaters and rivers – the River Thames froze and even the sea froze around the stanchions of Brighton Pier! At Redmire the ice was thick enough for a farmhand to drive a tractor across its frozen wastes.

Come the thaw and many thought Redmire Pool fish stocks had succumbed like many other waters had. Few carp had been spotted prior to the season start, and some reports claimed the pool was lifeless. Even though Pete Thomas landed a fine 20lb common in September 1963, many thought the place was finished, and in the years of 1964 and 1965 little angling took place at Redmire. The reign of the old Carp Catchers' Club was beginning to wane and people started looking to other waters that held big carp.

But all was about to change in the extraordinary story of Redmire Pool. In the spring of 1965 two keen specimen hunters, Bob Rolph and Grahame Igglesden, decided to find out where the hallowed pool was. To their credit they did just that, and upon entering the property over farm fields from the east they were suddenly confronted by the Redmire shallows. The most important thing about this event was the carp they saw – loads of them and some big ones too, so it seemed the stories about the carp dying in the freeze-up were unfounded.

Grahame Igglesden, who along with pal Bob Rolph, found out that the Redmire carp hadn't, as previously thought, perished in the mighty 1962/3 freeze-up.

After Bob Rolph and Grahame Igglesden made known that their visit had proved that the Redmire carp had survived the mighty freeze-up, notable carp angler John Nixon, himself the captor of a Redmire 23-pounder in 1961, made it possible for members of the major specimen groups at the time to fish at Redmire on a day ticket basis for the 1966 season.

Fresh minds and youthful energy were put to the test as new techniques and baits were tried at Redmire. Some great fish were caught, culminating in Devon Specimen Group member Roger Bowskill

One of the greats of the sport, Jack Hilton, with a glorious 23lb common from Redmire Pool in the summer of 1970.

landing a superb 38½lb mirror in September, the same fish that Eddie Price had caught in 1959.

The following September a gentleman who would have a strong association with Redmire Pool in coming years made a successful visit to the pool: his name was Jack Hilton. Jack caught a 35lb mirror on that trip and for the next eight years the pool totally dominated his life. There is little doubt in my mind that Redmire had Jack Hilton by the throat... his house was named Redmire Cottage, his business was named Redmire Landscapes (his son Keith still has the same company business and name) and from 1968 Jack ran a syndicate on Redmire until he gave up fishing in 1976.

How the press reported Bill Quinlan's record brace of carp from Redmire Pool in 1970.

Failure was not in Jack's vocabulary and he stated at the time that here (at Redmire) the syndicate had the biggest carp in the country to fish for. The rules governing the fishing in no way hindered anglers and with just ten trusted, dedicated carp anglers in the syndicate something was likely to happen – a record carp could be on the cards. And happen it did, once the days of potato and breadpaste were over and in came such delights as maggots, sultanas and ultimately sweetcorn.

The number of carp over twenty pounds that Redmire held at the time was impressive – how does sixty such fish sound, in just three acres?

The experiments in baits yielded amazing results, with people like Bill Quinlan, Tom Mintram and of course Jack Hilton catching numbers of twenty- and thirty-pounder carp in the early 1970s. However, in 1972 things were about to change again in the story of Redmire Pool.

Rod Hutchinson and Chris Yates

Two young carp anglers gained access to the syndicate at the time, Rod Hutchinson and Chris Yates. They brought a fresh and totally unfettered approach to the fishing at the mighty pool. With energy and

Rod Hutchinson enjoyed great success at Redmire (and everywhere else too!).

commitment plus a touch of quirkiness the pair ran roughshod over all that had happened before. It was the small particle approach that won the day for these Redmire anglers. Rod, ever the bait experimenter, tried all manner of baits including hemp (very successful), chickpeas, mini-maples, haricot beans, black-eyed beans, jelly babies (I kid you not), shrimps and God knows what else, while Chris threw in pigeon racing beans, mungo beans, aduki beans and the most successful of them all, sweetcorn.

The sweetcorn incident is worth recording. Chris had taken a tin of Jolly Green Giant sweetcorn with him to eat. It was opened one July morning in 1972 to form part of the filling for an omelette. Using half the contents for the said dish, it then struck Chris that it might be useful as a bait. He put a piece on the hook and threw it out. Within minutes he had a run; he put another piece on and had another run. Though the fish were small by Redmire standards, the bait showed promise...

Both Rod and Chris caught a great many carp from Redmire on particle baits that showed a way forward. This theme was rammed home by Kevin Clifford in 1975, when he landed an amazing nine 20lb carp in a week. The thing Kev did different was to work out the sheer amount of sweetcorn a single carp could consume. Gone were the days of a small can or two of corn – Kev went armed with catering-sized cans of the stuff!

The late 1970s saw the use of boilies at the pool for the first time. Successful Kent

A rare black and white picture of Chris Yates with his 51½lb record-breaker on opening day, 1980.

carper Roy Johnson used high-protein boilies to great effect, and then later Len Bunn and Dick Weale with their Black Majic amino acid-based boilies did the trick.

A New Record
Is there any better day to catch a record carp than opening day (when we had a close season, of course)? Well that's just what Chris Yates did on 16 June 1980, when he captured the country's first 50-pounder. It's a little-recorded fact that Redmire produced the first 30lb, 40lb and 50lb carp, but there again, we are talking about Redmire.

The capture of Chris Yates' 51½lb mirror was a giant step forward in the size anglers could expect carp in England to grow, yet now as I write over twenty-five years later we have an English record carp weighing over fifteen pounds more! Enough of Redmire for the moment... back to the plot!

DICK WALKER'S INFLUENCE – THE 1950s AND 60s

The methods that Richard Walker expounded about catching fish through his massive writing output (and a number of classic books) starting in the late 1940s changed the face of modern coarse fishing (and for that matter trout fishing as well). Here was an intelligent, articulate and educated person of great character who turned his mind to the pursuit (initially) of catching carp.

Dick Walker promoted a logical and scientific approach to his fishing, and so persuasive was he on the subject that he convinced others that carp were catchable by design, not just luck. This massive change of attitude was to have far-reaching effects. His influence also had a profound effect on rod design, electronic bite alarms, lead weights, carp hooks, methods and tactics.

Dick started his carp catching way back in the early 1930s, and between the years of 1933 and 1939 it has been stated he caught an astonishing fifty-three carp between ten and sixteen pounds. I can

Dick Walker promoted a logical and scientific approach to his fishing.

Just one fish from the remarkable catch of big carp taken from Billing Aquadrome by Bob Reynolds in 1957.

tried by a number of anglers who were new to carp fishing at the time, but were rewarded with big carp from the off. One such budding carp angler, Bob Atkinson, tried his luck at a lake near Southampton; he went on to land a number of carp over 20lb during a successful few years at the water, most falling for floating crust tactics.

A top ten of carp captured in 1952 shows the yawning gap between Walker's record 44-pounder and other big carp captured that year:

44lb	Richard Walker	Redmire Pool
28lb 10oz	Pete Thomas	Redmire Pool
25lb	Ken Drayton	Butt's Pond
24lb 12oz	Maurice Ingham	Redmire Pool
22lb 12oz	Richard Walker	Dagenham
22lb 8oz	Robert Atkinson	Stoneham
20lb 7½oz	Robert Atkinson	Stoneham
20lb	Fred Bull	Dagenham
19lb 12½oz	Robert Atkinson	Stoneham
19lb	Bernard Venables	Goffs Park

think of no other person who had landed so many double-figure carp at the time, so clearly he knew what he was talking about.

In June 1951, on the dam at Mapperley, four anglers assembled for a carp fishing holiday. They were Dick Walker, Maurice Ingham, 'BB' and John Norman. During conversation, the subject of a club for carp anglers came up. The ramifications of what was to be called the Carp Catchers' Club would provide a real milestone in the successful pursuit of catching big carp. A few months later, Bob Richards' capture of a 31¼lb carp, as I have already written of, sent shock waves through the angling world and its consequences were to be felt for the next twenty-five years in carp fishing.

One method championed by Walker was margin fishing for carp with floating crust. During the early to mid-1950s this was

In contrast to the overwhelming season of 1952, the following year proved to be an anticlimax, with Carp Catchers' Club member Gerry Berth-Jones banking the only 20-pounder – a grand 23lb 10oz mirror from Dagenham.

But after this, things moved at a pace, with the middle years of the 1950s seeing 20lb carp coming from places as far flung as Manchester, Sussex, Birmingham, Middlesex and Bedfordshire. More and more anglers were taking up carp fishing as they realized that careful thought together with the correct tackle could net them a big carp.

At the same time, carp were getting bigger and anglers were increasingly being seduced into trying waters that had a reputation as being impossible to approach because of the 'uncatachable' tag of the carp stocks. A nice illustration of this hap-

The highly successful carp catcher Elliott Symack with a carp from Peterborough's Electricity Cut in the late 1960s.

pened in 1957, when a young shoe shop manager, Bob Reynolds, wrote his name into the record books with a string of big carp from previously unknown carp water, Billing Aquadrome, near Northampton.

Walker's doctrine was first find the fish, don't scare them, use tackle broadly suited to the situation you find, fish with a bait they will eat, angle at the right time … and bingo! Though fishing is never as easy as this, it's a winning formula that has been used by thousands of successful anglers ever since. Bob Reynolds' spectacular catches in August 1957 meant he'd landed the sixth, seventh and eighth largest carp ever, besides being the first angler to land

two carp over 20lb in the same session. In 1961 Bob accounted for another whopper from Billing in the shape of a 33lb 2oz mirror.

By the end of the 1950s the pursuit of fishing for carp had grown to a level where tackle companies starting to advertise rods and reels aimed specifically at the carp angler. It was the era of 10ft, 1½lb TC rods and Mitchell 300 reels, monofil line and heavyweight hooks. As the 1960s unfolded, split cane as a rod-making material gave way to fibreglass, monofil lines became more reliable and a great many of the more practical anglers started making purpose-built electronic bite alarms, large landing nets and more and more adaptations of carp rods – fibreglass giving far more scope than the earlier split cane material.

Headline-grabbing catches of big carp became more prevalent, with thirty-pounders coming from Tiddenfoot pit and the Electricity Cut, the latter being an off-shoot channel off the River Nene near Peterborough, Northants, which benefited from volumes of warm water being discharged from the turbines of the local electricity power station (now long gone).

Other Big Carp

Many lakes in Kent that had been stocked with fast-growing carp some years before starting to produce wonderful catches to the likes of fast-rising stars such as Gerry Savage, Jim Gibbinson, Mike Harris and Bruce Ashby.

After a numbers of years, two 40lb carp were captured during the 1966 season, neither being from Redmire pool. The biggest, a 42lb common, came from the by now famous Billing Aquadrome, the other, a 40½lb mirror from a Hertfordshire pit called Westbrook Mere. Ron Groombridge, a young apprentice carpenter who lived nearby, had the carp bug (real bad) and knew this local lake held some whoppers. To his credit he targeted these fish and one July evening his floating crust was taken by a monster. Redmire Pool, which had taken a back seat for a while, came back with a bang with fish of 38½lb in 1966 and 35lb in 1967, each landed by expert carp anglers of the period, Roger Bowskill and the redoubtable Jack Hilton.

It was this period, the late 1960s, that saw an influx of young and determined men hell bent on catching ever larger carp. With fresh minds they reached out to catch their dreams, and many succeeded (but also thousands did not). However, progress was made. Take winter fishing for example.

This really took off in the late 1960s. Anglers such as Kent's Gerry Savage were catching more double-figure fish in the winter months than most other carp anglers did in the summertime! Gerry, along with Jim Gibbinson, Mike Winter, Keith Dickens and Elliott Symack, wrote extensively about cold-water carp catching, which spurred on many, including the author, to try their hand. Now, forty years later, some truly huge fish have been landed in the depths of winter, including record carp.

THE 1970s

During the early 1970s Redmire Pool was yet again the dominant force in producing huge carp. The likes of Jack Hilton, Bill Quinlan, Tom Mintram, Chris Yates, Rod Hutchinson and others showed that maggots and small particle-sized baits were a way forward in outwitting the normally super-cautious Redmire carp. Tremendous catches of carp were taken at the time, Redmire alone producing new record braces of carp to Bill Quinlan and later John MacLeod in this period.

Again, thousands of new hopefuls were joining the ranks of carp fishing. The availability of worthwhile waters holding decent carp were growing as each season went by. Tackle and tactics were becoming more and more refined and baits were being much more closely investigated. The likes of luncheon meat, sausage paste, Kit-e-Kat and other pet foods, and eventually trout pellets were proving effective the country over. These were initially known as 'specials', and when the idea took off of boiling those baits that had eggs in their make-up that formed an outer skin, the term 'boilies' became the name that has stuck ever since. The ingredients in boilies went through a revolution when Fred Wilton, a docker from East London, developed a recipe of milk protein-based powder blended with vitamins and minerals to form a highly nutritious bait, which, once sampled by the carp, was then searched out by them when on the feed. Fred Wilton's high-nutrient value (HNV) baits started to take waters apart and those first on his mixes (his friends) enjoyed unparalleled catches at the time. I can think of many successful carp anglers who fell under Fred's spell, including Bob Morris, Robin Munday, Steve Edwards and even the great Jim Gibbinson.

Though there was a great deal of debate at the time as to the validity of Fred's theories and bait, we know with hindsight that he was dead right. Simply put, Fred Wilton unlocked the door to the now vast world of baits and ingredients, which has become a major business with carp fishing.

From 1974 onwards the size of carp being caught could be gauged by surveying the big carp lists of the period. You needed to catch a carp above 31¼lb to get into the top ten from the mid-1970s onwards. One-time ace carp catcher from Kent, Roy Johnson, appeared five times in the top ten captures for the seasons of 1975 and 1976 – quite a remarkable achievement. Anglers of note who also started to appear with big carp under their belt included Rod Hutchinson, Clive Diedrich, Derek Richie, the late Vic Gillings, Ritchie McDonald, Keith Cayzer and Bruce Ashby, among others.

The availability of carp fishing venues had never been better and a number of the top anglers who had tasted great success already were starting to look at big, windswept gravel pits, waters that had a reputation of containing big carp where few, if any, anglers had yet appeared on the bank. One such fisherman, Peter Springate, showed what the potential of places such as these could be. In 1978 he astounded the carp world with the biggest ever brace of carp at the time, and it's worth spending a little time looking at this famous capture.

Peter Springate

Peter Springate has been a part of the carp fishing community as long as most people can remember. Like many, he started fishing as a kid and went through the massive learning curve that sadly few youngsters these days enjoy. By the time Pete turned to carp fishing he'd sampled the delights of catching minnows, gudgeon, roach, rudd, tench, crucians, perch and bream. By the early 1970s he had became besotted by carp, and like many of that period, wanted to catch more and larger carp. This was a time of big breakthroughs in carp fishing, as waters holding big carp, especially large gravel pits that had seen little in the way of any angling pressure, let alone from carp anglers, were starting to come under scrutiny.

Pete and his constant angling companion, Ken Hodder, lived in south London, which afforded them easy access to Surrey, Sussex and Kent waters. If they ventured further west and then north, close to the outskirts of London, they came to the start of the Thames Valley and the Colne Valley. Here there were gravel pits, some of which were massive and many that subsequently became famous carp waters: Wraysbury 1 and 2, Rayners, Kingsmead, Longfield, Silverwings, Colnmere, Horton, then further along the M4 corridor, Summerleaze, Englefield Lagoon, Farnham Flint, Burefield, Sonning Eye, Tarmac, White Swan, the Causeway and so on. The big pits close to Heathrow Airport at Staines particularly attracted Pete and Ken; one with the unusual name of Yeoveney started to become increasingly appealing as it seemed to have all the right ingredients to produce really big fish.

Yeoveney Pit

Yeoveney Pit was stocked with carp from way back, though I have never been able to establish with any certainty who stocked what and when into the vast waters of this gravel pit, which was still being worked in the early 1970s.

At a guess, there might have been around forty carp or so that made the transition safely from small fish to become adult carp. Come 1968–70, most of these were twenty-pounders, and the sight of them had attracted one or two keen-eyed fishermen – one such angler was Colin Claydon. Colin, along with others, formed a dedicated band of followers of these carp. They were extremely hard to catch and represented a real feather in your cap if you did succeed. Colin Claydon, in particular, had a couple of exceptional seasons, landing no fewer than thirteen twenty-pounders plus others close to that weight.

The mighty Tom Mintram, carp lake hunter extraordinaire, found Yeoveney and fished there along with his son Mike and another carp angler of note, John Carver. Around this time the late Chris Seager was another who became bewitched by Yeoveney, as were Martin Moyers and Dave Goy. Some caught; others dreamed of catching... such was the fascination of the venue.

By the late 1970s some of the earlier carp anglers had drifted away and Yeoveney became quiet again and a comparatively unfished water. The carp still thrived, however, and some by now had grown into very big fish. It was no coincidence that Pete Springate and Ken Hodder appeared on the scene at this time. They had done their homework and knew what the pit had produced in the past; maybe there were some real lunkers swimming about now ... The pair decided to find out more.

By this time the Surrey/Middlesex region of the British Carp Study Group had become well established. Being its regional organizer from the off I came into contact with a wealth of carp fishing talent including the likes of Tom Mintram, Mike Mintram, Ritchie McDonald, Chris Seager, Roy Johnson, Mike Starkey, Vic Gillings, John Carver, Joe Jarman, Clive Diedrich, Malcolm Winkworth, Chris Yates, Pete and Ken and a host of others. Our monthly meetings at the Crooked Billet pub just outside Staines were perfect for Pete Springate and Ken Hodder, as they could bait up at Yeoveney on the way to the meetings – and they often did. Pete takes up the story:

> It was Thursday 26 October 1978, and I had just finished work at midday and was eager to get down to the lake for the weekend. I had a strong feeling that I would catch a fish this weekend. The events of the last two weeks had given me a lot of confidence. I had caught my second carp from the lake two weeks before, a lovely looking mirror of 24lb, which gave a fantastic fight – in the end I had to go in and lift it out with my hands.
>
> Then last weekend I saw a lot of carp in the area, some leaping clear of the water others just head-and-shouldering, much more activity than I had seen all season. I had spent most weekends and three to four nights a week on the lake and had in all that time only seen about six fish, so I could not wait to get back. I had been down on the Tuesday evening and put some bait in on my way to our BCSG meeting at Staines.

When Pete arrived he found the gate locked near where he wanted to fish so had to park his van by the main entrance to the old pit workings. After climbing over the fence and getting his gear over, he walked the mile or so round to the point where he intended to fish. No one else had been fishing the lake all season except for Ken Hodder, who had just returned from Somerset the day before. When he arrived at his spot the wind was blowing from right to left – a moderate north-westerly.

Before setting his rods up he had to drag out masses of weed that had drifted into the swim. Pete used three rods, all 12ft Jack Hilton fast taper models, and Mitchell reels loaded with 10lb breaking strain line that was specially dyed. Baits were cast out twenty yards to a bar about twenty feet deep. The depth of water in the margins was about fifteen to eighteen feet. Pete carefully put three baits around each hook and then sat back and made a cup of tea. As it started to get dark, at about 6pm, the wind dropped and the lake became a flat calm; it was cloudy and very mild. Pete continues:

At about 7pm I heard a carp leap further along to my right. I picked up my binoculars to see if I could see any rings on the surface where it had leapt and started to wonder whether I should have set up in the swim I cut out the week before in the bushes further along, when my oscillator sounded. I put the binoculars down and could see the indicator on my second rod moving steadily up. I stood over the rod and the indicator stopped half way, and then carried on to the butt.

I struck hard and was into a fish that went off like a rocket to my right. It was going so fast that I just could not keep up back-winding with it and was forced to let the reel handle go. I knew there was a big weed bed further up the lake and also knew that I had to stop it from getting there, so I grabbed the reel handle and held on.

Because of the speed the fish went off Pete thought it must weigh fifteen to sixteen pounds; after all, the 24-pounder went off fast, but this one went twice as fast. After he gained some line the rod kicked over and was nearly wrenched from his hands as the fish went off once again. He remembers the corks creaking under his hand and thought the line or the rod was going to break at any moment.

Then everything went solid as the fish reached the weed bed. Pete kept the tension on as hard as he could and looked up at the rod tip. He saw that it moved back an inch, then another inch. After some minutes out on the surface a big mass of weed appeared, he placed the landing net in the water under the weed where he thought the fish was and lifted – then realized it was not in the net! Pete could see the fish was further away and thought if he could lift the 24-pounder out with his hands he could do the same again. As he touched it the water exploded, sending a shower over him. The fish decided it wanted to go out into the open water again, but Pete managed to get it back to the bank and then caught sight of its size – it had to be over thirty pounds. Eventually, after further problems, the fish was netted. Pete continues the story:

I parted the netting and could see that it was a good thirty. After unhooking it I got the large weigh bag, scales and torch. The scales went down to 32lb with a bang. I did not have my larger scales with me as I normally do because my van had been broken into a few weeks before and I had left them at home. I sacked the fish and went to telephone Ken, but he was out, so I left a message saying that I had caught a thirty and would he come and photograph it. Then I phoned my dad and asked him to go round to my place and bring my big scales down.

On my way back I stopped at a pub for a pint. I think everyone in the pub was

A famous picture of Peter Springate's remarkable record brace of carp – 36½lb (holding) and 38½lb.

staring at me because I was still shaking badly and had trouble trying to roll a cigarette! I got back to my rods and tied a new hook on and cast out again, and sat waiting for the scales.

Pete's Mum and Dad came along around 9pm and the fish was accurately weighed at 36½lb, Pete's first thirty. He thought he'd have to wait a long time for another like it – but fate had a further surprise waiting!

Before Pete could think any further he had another bite. He struck and was into another fish, which this time did not tear off, but held deep. He kept on pumping and pumping until finally it broke the surface two rod lengths out. He put as much pressure on as possible, slid the landing net into the water and brought the fish over it and straight in.

Pete remembers staggering up the bank thinking that this fish was even heavier than the last one, and when he put it down on the grass he could see a huge bulging carp in the net. Pete recalls:

I parted the mesh and thought, it's a forty! I unhooked it, got my big scales and tried to weigh it but I just could not keep the needle steady. It kept hovering around the forty pound mark. There were no decent trees around that I could hang the scales on so I had to sack the fish and wait for Ken to turn up in the morning.

I looked at my watch and it was 11.45pm: two thirty-pounders in four and a half hours! I did not get any sleep that night and at eight in the morning I had another take – I struck, but didn't feel anything. What a night, three takes, two fish, after all the time I had spent here without so much as a bleep from the oscillators.

Ken turned up at 9am and asked what the weight of the fish was. Pete asked him,

'Which one, the first or the second?' Ken looked in disbelief. When the sack was opened with the big one in, the pair could not believe their eyes – it was enormous and weighed 38½lb.

Peter Springate had landed the largest brace of carp ever at the time and many, including the author, thought it just reward for one of the most dedicated and successful carp anglers of modern times.

THE 1980s

As exciting as the 1970s had been, carp fishing was yet again going to crank it up a notch or two at the start of the next decade. The opening day of the 1980 season was a happy one for a number of anglers, including the author. First, Chris Yates landed a new record carp from Redmire Pool. The fish had tripped up as the evening light was slowing turning to dusk. Chris, true to form, crept up to the Redmire shallows with his 10ft split-cane, Avon-style rod, a tub of sweetcorn and a small ball of Plasticine (used as a weight). Fish were showing on Redmire's shallows that evening, and though big fish showed close to where he had cast, nothing happened until he noticed a big dark shape moving close to the bank just where a small willow tree hung over the water. In a deft move Chris silently flicked his bait into the path of the fish. Within moments it made off with the sweetcorn and a dramatic battle ensued, the shallow water erupting with the disturbance. On hearing the commotion, colleagues John Carver and Barry Mills were soon at Chris' side and provided essential help. His luck held and sometime after the fish was hooked, John Carver slipped the net under what was clearly a big fish.

Weighed on the bank, the monster pulled the scales down to 51lb 6oz. The

Here I am with a twenty-pounder on opening day 1980 from Yateley's Match Lake.

scales were later checked by the Weights and Measures Department in Guildford, Surrey, and found to be weighing 2oz light, so the true weight of the UK's first fifty-pounder was 51½lb. It's a little-known fact that Chris had landed this same carp some seven years earlier at 38lb again on sweetcorn.

On the same day, way over in the Colne Valley, a small syndicate of carp anglers were let loose on a large gravel pit close to Denham which had a reputation for harbouring large carp. Indeed, this place, Savay, had seen some spectacular catches made by Mike Wilson in the mid- to late-1970s, though these had been kept very hush-hush.

When the likes of Rod Hutchinson, Andy Little and Lenny Middleton started on their campaign at Savay, incredible catches were soon made. Savay contained large numbers of carp over 20lb, besides a healthy number of fish over 30lb... it was a time of plenty. I always remember Rod Hutchinson telling me about frantic trips he'd make to a local telephone box along the road from the fishery (this of course was years before mobile phones) and ringing the weatherman. 'When are we going to get some wind?' or, 'Is there a low pressure looming?' These questions meant a lot to those fishing at Savay. If a change of wind direction was due within twenty-four hours Rod would move his pitch to be where the wind was going to blow. He would then pile the bait in and wait for the fish to move on the wind. Andy Little did the same, and on one occasion banked four fish, three of them over 30lb! Savay influence is still felt today, over twenty-five years later, as the place is teeming with big fish and a few years ago even produced its first fifty-pounder.

Also on the same day – 16 June 1980 – I was fishing at a lake that was largely unknown at the time, and though it was the start of the season, few anglers were about; in fact I might have been the only one to cast in at midnight.

By 6.30am on an overcast opening morning, I'd landed a brace of twenty-pounders and also met someone who would become an angling buddy ever since. His name was Jan Wenczka, the water was the Yateley Match lake. Like Savay, the Yateley complex on the Surrey/Hampshire border was to become a famous venue over the years for its carp stocks.

New Developments

Around this time two anglers, Len Middleton and Kevin Maddocks, starting looking at ways to deal with something that drove carp anglers mad at the time, 'twitch bites'. Side hooking – where the point of a hook was proud of the bait, usually a boilie – helped, but it was Lenny and Kevin who hit on the idea of attaching the bait to a fine link and tying this link, 'the hair', to the bend of the hook: the hair-rig was born.

The word on this rig got out slowly (I first heard of it in the late summer of 1981). Used correctly and cast into feeding areas, it revolutionized catches and sometimes made catching carp, including big fish, seem easy. The effect of the hair-rig is such that now, more twenty-five years later, few carp anglers (or other big fish anglers for that matter) would ever consider casting out a bait without attaching it to some sort of hair rig... this amazing concept that has stood the test of time.

The early 1980s saw the birth of a new organization for carp anglers, the Carp Society. At the same time came a breathtaking publication, *Carp Fisher*, the likes of which had no equals at the time in terms of design and production. The fact that a new outfit could come up with such a swanky publication provoked a sharp intake of breath from the monthly magazines at the time, many of which were printed solely in black and white on relatively poor quality paper. *Carp Fisher* started a revolution in the fishing magazine printing world, but it took a time for the rest to catch up. The Carp Society meanwhile grew from strength to strength and became active at all levels, setting up terrific conferences and a network of regional meetings that saw well-known and successful carp anglers give slide shows and talks. The Society also had a political involvement in angling.

The 1980s was another period of tremendous growth in carp fishing influenced greatly by the publication of two milestone carp angling books, Rod Hutchinson's *Carp Book* and Kevin Maddocks' *Carp Fever*. These two books almost single-handedly changed the face of carp fishing forever. Both were full of new ideas and information on tackle, tactics, baits and understanding the quarry. On one hand you had Rod Hutchinson explaining just what catches were possible by using particle baits and the whole thinking behind his fantastic methods. Also for the first time Rod exposed anglers to a 'spod', a 'throwing stick' and the use of PVA. Rod's reputation at the time was sky high; his catches were just outrageous wherever he went. His writings were also amusing, which made all his later books turn into bestsellers. Though he took his fishing seriously he was hardly what I would call an organized angler. He didn't have to have his rods in perfect spirit-level straightness and though the fishing was enjoyable, so too was the pub and the curry house. Indeed Rod wrote almost as much about this side of his fishing as he did about his catches.

Kevin Maddocks, on the other hand, waged a war on carp with an almost military precision. Why, there was a two-page picture feature in *Carp Fever* which showed you how to strike a fish while lying down on a bedchair, get out and put on your footwear without losing what was attached to the end of your line… brilliant! Besides containing vital information, just like Rod's book, on tackle, tactics and bait, Kevin Maddocks made fashion statements too. Within a year or two of *Carp Fever* being published, you just weren't a serious carp angler unless you went fishing in a green army jumper with shoulder patches (I had one too!). Kevin Maddocks also championed a reel that was to take over from the mighty Mitchell 300 and 410 that had for so long ruled as the carp angler's mainstay reel. In all the pictures, and featured heavily in *Carp Fever*, was the ABU Cardinal 55 fixed spool reel. This all-black reel with gold decal

markings was, and still is, a beauty (I still have three 55s from 1979, the year they were introduced.)

These two anglers led the way during the early 1980s, but there was a wealth of other talent in carp fishing at the time – the likes of Roy Johnson, Bruce Ashby, Jim Gibbinson, Ritchie McDonald, Andy Little, Clive Deidrich, Bob Morris and Chris Yates.

Ritchie McDonald

Of these anglers, the capture by Ritchie McDonald of the second-largest carp caught at the time, a massive 45¾lb mirror caught in October 1984 from the North Lake on the Yateley complex, sparked many of the top carp anglers of today into big carp hunters forever. I'd like to dwell on this capture because it was such an important point in carp fishing history.

Though Ritchie McDonald has faded from the scene nowadays, I can't begin to tell you how big a figure he was in the carp world a quarter of a century ago. He had come through the ranks, fishing at Ashlea, Redmire, Longfield, Savay, the Cons, Wraysbury and beyond. He was fantastically successful plus being what some people would call a colourful figure, which made him seem larger than life to the general angling public. When he had his 'fishing head' on, and I knew him through those successful years, he was simply unstoppable.

Ritchie's thoughts on carp fishing at the time he caught the North Lake fish were simple. I quote: 'Carp anglers want to catch big fish for the same reason that mountaineers want to climb high mountains – because they are there. When they've caught a twenty they want to catch a thirty and when they've done that, they want to catch a forty.'

This is what happened in Ritchie's case. Listen to this from the man himself: 'I remember the day I decided to try for the big Yateley fish; I can even smell the fried mushrooms on Roger Smith's plate. We – Roger, Rod Hutchinson and myself – were in the cafe near Savay, getting stuck into full breakfasts, that is, bacon, eggs, tomatoes, sausages, fried bread, beans, toast and marmalade and two pots of tea – and in Roger's case, fried mushrooms whenever he had had a fish the day before.'

In between mouthfuls, Rod was flicking through *Anglers' Mail* and he stopped to admire the famous Yateley North Lake fish, caught at 43lb by a tench angler. Rod asked Ritchie if he'd seen the picture; he wasn't interested because it was such a 'big ugly bugger.' Rod replied, 'You must be joking,' showing Ritchie the paper … who had to agree he was wrong, it was a handsome-looking carp. Rod and Ritchie just looked at each other and Ritchie said, 'Shall we go for it?'

The campaign the pair mounted required all of Ritchie's undoubted carp-catching skills to come to the fore as he became more and more embroiled in the catching of this one carp.

Quest for the North Lake Carp

They decided to start in August 1984 and enlisted the help of a local carp angler, Richard Everson, who was going to join them. He had a couple of young mates, Mark Cox and John North, who were happy to make the bait for Ritchie and Rod. They gave the lads the Hutchy Protein Mix and Pukka Salmon flavour (a real winner at the time) and told them which areas to bait up two weeks before they were to arrive. They used twelve pounds of bait over those two weeks – two pounds at each visit.

Ritchie went down to have a look at the lake and liked a spot called the Christmas Tree swim; it was where the fish had been caught before.

However, plans hit a snag when Rod rang to say his wife was ill and that he wouldn't be able to make it, so with Richard Everson joining later, Ritchie went on his own. He arrived on 22 August – a good time to begin serious carp fishing, as he'd found in the past – just before the fish begin their heavy autumn feeding.

That first session lasted five days, but the second visit was over in twenty-four hours. Ritchie wrote about this at the time, giving an insight into his level of understanding of the art of catching big fish. 'It just didn't feel right or look right. There didn't seem to be a movement anywhere in the water or on the land; even the birds seemed quiet and the lake was flat calm. There's only one thing to do when it's like that and that's to pack up and go home.'

On his third visit Ritchie got there late and only had time to set up and cast out before darkness fell. The Christmas Tree area had been free so he had dropped in there. Lying half asleep, a golden-coloured carp leapt thirty yards out and along to his right and then fell back with a crash. His glimpse of the fish and the ripples it sent across the lake told him it was a good'un. An hour later he had a run and landed a beautiful, golden mirror of 23¾lb – he believed it was the same fish he had seen.

On the next visit Richard Everson fished too. Ritchie started on the Christmas Tree but was keen to try other areas in case he was missing something, and when two fish crashed out during the night at the other end of the lake, he packed up and was on his way round soon after first light.

Feeling like a stroll the next morning, he went to see an angler he knew who was fishing opposite the point and he mentioned in passing that he'd heard a fish jump in the night. 'It was like a cow falling in,' he said, but had hardly got the

What a tremendous capture and one that inspired so many anglers at the time – Ritchie McDonald with his Yateley North Lake monster of 45¾lb.

words out when Ritchie started giving an ear-bending for not saying something sooner.

It was halfway through October when he decided it was time for one last effort before fishing became really unpleasant and his chances disappeared. Nothing happened on Friday night, but on Saturday morning at 11.30am Richard landed the golden 23lb fish Ritchie had banked a few weeks before, and things were looking better all the time. On Saturday night Ritchie couldn't sleep.

When Sunday morning dawned there was still an electric atmosphere around the lake, as if everything was holding its

breath, and this kept going throughout the day. At 7pm he had a run. Picking up the rod and striking, he instinctively knew what he had hooked. The fish started moving slowly, steadily and powerfully away from the island where it had picked up the bait, then it kited parallel to the bank. Ritchie pulled it towards the snag and, like most fish you hook, it responded to the pressure by swimming in the opposite direction and into open water.

From then on, steady pressure with 8lb line brought it slowly towards him and in less than five minutes it was ready for the net. No one had said a word until then and Ritchie broke the silence only to ask Geoff to pass him the landing net. A few seconds later it was in the net.

Back to Ritchie: 'Geoff read the scales and announced 47lb 4oz, which, with a quick calculation of minus 1½lb for the weigh bag, left a weight of 45lb 12oz.' Until then Ritchie had just wanted to catch a 40lb carp. He soon realized he'd done quite a bit more: in the sack was the second heaviest carp ever landed in Britain.

Ritchie went back to the lake that night but couldn't sleep. Fish were crashing out in front of him yet he didn't cast out. He was content with what he'd caught and wasn't interested in catching anything else.

The next morning everyone arrived. Photos were taken and even a video and then it was down to the Fisheries pub near Savay for a pint and to organize a celebration. It was all arranged for Monday night. An evening in the pub, a meal in the Tandoori House and then back to Rod's bivvy at Savay, where they all talked into the night.

The video of the weighing, photographing and returning of the fish revealed Ritchie's delight as he stood by the water with arms in the air and fists clenched, letting out a tremendous victory shout. (I have a copy of this video, one of only a handful that were reproduced, and now, 25 years later, possibly the only one left!)

The Late 1980s

By 1986 the very young Julian Cundiff had started to make a name for himself. His writing output on all matters related to carp fishing during the next 15 years was truly amazing. Julian, like many before him, sparked the fire in many young anglers who were soon to become carp anglers.

An important event happened in early June 1988. It was announced earlier that year by the Carp Society that a special

Richard Walker Remembrance Conference would be held to celebrate fifty years of carp fishing. This remarkable event embraced many of Dick's old friends and his family, and was an outstanding success and a major triumph for organizer Mike Kavanagh and the Carp Society. Then, to cap it all, it was announced that the Society had gained control of famous Redmire Pool through the sterling work of Les Bamford – and Les continues to run the fishing to this day.

The year 1988 was also significant for a number of new carp books, including Rod Hutchinson's *Carp Now and Then*, Tim Paisley's first two books, *Carp Fishing* and *Carp Season* and Rob Maylin's first book, *Tiger Bay*. In addition, *Carpworld* became the first newsstand carp magazine ever, first published in August 1988.

The late 80s also saw Rob Maylin become the darling of the carp world. His amazing catches and successful books made him a household name. Rob struck me as a 'relaxed' version of Ritchie McDonald. He came from a match-fishing background and went on for a number of years as one of the dominant forces in carp fishing. Though he waned a little as the new millennium approached, he has reappeared in force during the last few years.

CARP IN THE MEDIA – THE 1990s

Throughout the 1990s, carp magazines were a prime indicator of the growth of carp fishing: *Carp Fisher* moved from being six-monthly to bi-monthly, while *Carpworld* went from bi-monthly to monthly. In April 1991 Rob Maylin started publishing his own magazine, *Big Carp*. Then perhaps the most startling publishing event happened – on 18 June 1994 a weekly carp paper/magazine became a

Though full of controversy at the time, the fact remained that Roddy Porter caught a potential new record carp of 53lb 15oz in early June 1995.

reality with the birth of *Carp-Talk*. This 64-page publication entered the marketplace in competition with a thirty-year-old and forty-year-old product already established. But the massive rollercoaster of carp fishing saw that the weekly was here to stay. Now a dozen years later it's still the main source for all that is happening in the carp world on a week-to-week basis. The magazine's popularity made the *Angler's Mail* and *Angling Times* sit up and take notice, and they too had to find ways to cater for what was obviously an expanding market.

Carp fishing even spread to TV in the mid-1990s, when the highly acclaimed *Passion for Angling* series was broadcast by the BBC; the series had plenty on carp fishing.

Many venues became famous for their truly huge carp stocks during the 1990s. It would take another chapter the size of this one to list all the big carp caught during the final decade of the last century. But here are some of the highlights: Savay lake produced whopping braces of carp to the likes of Max Cottis and Albert Romp (the largest of each brace weighed well over 40lb). The Yateley North Lake mirror (which Ritchie caught in 1984) was still growing, with Don Orris recording a weigh of 46lb 1oz in June 1991. A month later Pete Springate stunned the carp world with a monster 45lb 6oz mirror from Wraysbury (more on this fish in a moment), while in 1992 Dave Cumpstone landed Britain's second 50lb carp from Wraysbury. Another much-coveted carp from a secret Colne Valley water made an appearance at 45¼lb to Jason Haywood, and in December 1994 one of the carp world's most likable, respected and successful anglers, Martin Locke, banked the third 50lb carp from the UK.

The year of 1995 turned into a watershed for fishing in general, for it was the first year that the old close season was abolished. Clubs, associations and riparian owners of stillwaters had for the first time the right to open or close their waters at any time during the year, and many opted for all-year fishing. Almost straightaway controversy was caused by Roddy Porter catching a record carp in the 'old close season'. This carp weighed 53lb 15oz, and was landed again within a week or so (in season this time) by Alex White at 55¼lb. The clearly spawnbound fish later died.

I haven't yet had much to say about the growth of carp-fishing books, especially in the 1990s. The prolific pen of Tim Paisley accounted for four books published, *Big Carp*, *Carp Amid the Storm*, *From the Bivvy* and *To Catch a Carp*; Kev Clifford's superb *A History of Carp Fishing* was published in 1992 and I had my book, *The King Carp Waters*, published in 1993. Others that were greeted with critical acclaim were Phil Thompson's *Waiting for Waddle*, Dave Lane's *An Obsession with Carp*, Terry Hearn's *In Pursuit of the Largest*, Paul Selman's *Carp Reflections*, and perhaps the most remarkable of the lot, Jim Gibbinson's latest carp work, *Gravel Pit Carp*. It was Jim's fifth carp-only book over a forty-year time span, an unprecedented achievement.

Mention of Terry Hearn reminds me of the great happenings that befell this young angler in November 1996. After becoming adept at catching some of the biggest carp around, Terry went straight to the top of the heap when he caught one of the country's most famous carp from one of the most famous UK lakes, and this turned out to be a new record carp as well. The fish was named Mary, the venue was Wraysbury No. 1 and the weight 55lb 13oz. Incidentally, to get into the top ten recorded captures of 1996 you had to catch a carp weighing at least 50lb 5oz. Such were the sizes of carp being caught.

Even the neglected art of surface fishing for carp had come of age as the end of the millennium dawned, for at least twenty-five carp weighing 35lb or more had been landed, most during the last decade of the millennium.

THE NEW MILLENNIUM

The massive growth of carp fishing in the last five years has seen maybe as many as 70,000 disciples in the UK alone going carp fishing. The statistics of catches are truly mind-boggling, as are the size of the carp in this country nowadays. I could cite any number of worthy stories of big carp caught in recent times, but to illustrate this I can do no better than to tell of the capture of a huge brace of fish that I was personally involved with and that *Carp-Talk* exclusively reported on.

Summerleaze Stunners

Martin Clarke has landed many fine carp from a variety of difficult waters over the years. He is a dedicated big carp angler who puts a great deal into his fishing. He knew of Summerleaze, it being in the vicinity of his old stomping ground and another gravel pit of note – the famous Taplow Lake in Berkshire. The stock of carp in Summerleaze was low compared to the sixty-odd acres of water; however, a few had grown into very big fish.

The carp themselves were reputed to be of the distinguished Galician race supplied by Donald Leney. Though I have never found (sadly) a reference to carp being stocked into Summerleaze in any of the old Surrey Trout Farm and United Fisheries' (Donald Leney's company) invoice books certainly some of these big Summerleaze fish (I've seen a few from the lake over the years) do have a Leney look about them.

Since Summerleaze is primarily a boating lake, anglers were at one stage restricted to a mere few hundred yards of bank, but then the opportunity to fish from an island was made available to syndicate members. It was from the second island that Martin made his historic catch of mirrors weighing 45½lb and 46lb 2oz in June 2000.

The dramatic nature of these captures was heightened by a series of mobile phone calls by Martin to Simon Crow at the *Carp-Talk* offices. When he landed the first mirror, a fantastically long and beautifully proportioned 45½lb fish, he rang Simon at our office. Within minutes Simon rang me to ask whether I could drive to Summerleaze to take some photos and get the story. The lake was 45 minutes to an hour away, so I made haste straightaway and within five minutes or so was in the car and heading for Berkshire. The traffic always seems worse when you are in a rush, and this day was no different, I just seemed to get held up at every junction or set of traffic lights.

About halfway into the journey my mobile rang, and the now slightly high-pitched and excited voice of Simon Crow blurted out, 'Chris, Chris, you're never going to believe this, but I've got Martin Clarke on the other phone here and he's looking down on another fish in his landing net which looks as big as the first one!'

I pulled over quickly, raising a couple of angry beeps from the disgruntled driver behind, 'What!' I exclaimed. Simon continued, 'It's true – Martin's telling me he's got the big fully scaled in the net as we speak and it's massive … what a catch, two whackers like this inside an hour.'

I restarted my journey still thwarted by heavy traffic, which I took little notice of, my mind being full of enormous carp. It was sometime later that I eventually made it to Summerleaze. Once inside the gate I met syndicate leader Richard and together we walked around to the furthest point, where we waited for Martin to come across in the boat.

Sure enough, within minutes he appeared, coming from a distant island. We scrabbled aboard. 'Well done, mate – what are these fish like?' I asked. 'I still can't quite believe it, Chris, two fish like that, both of them lake records, wait till you see them,' Martin excitedly told me as the boat chugged off towards the island.

Soon we were on dry land again, and once everything was prepared, the moment came to see the monstrous beasties, starting with the 45½lb mirror. It was a totally classic big carp, and I've been lucky to be in the presence of a few such carp over the years – this one was up with the best of them. But I guess the star of the show had to be the heavily scaled 46lb 2oz mirror. Though not as perfectly shaped as the other mirror, because of the scaling it was without doubt far more striking.

Here are Martin's words on this extraordinary catch, taken from his much acclaimed book, *Strictly Carp* (Bountyhunter Publications, 2001):

Just as I was settling into some writing one of my right-hand rods burst into life. I was onto it straight away and with the rod taking on a nice curve I instantly knew that it was another big carp as it kited right. As quick as I could I put on my lifejacket and pushed the boat out. Slowly I made my way towards the carp, gaining line as I went. Fifteen minutes later I got my first sighting and it looked huge as it swam past four to five feet below the surface.

The power and strength the carp showed was incredible as it insisted on staying deep for a further ten minutes before it had finally had enough and came into the upper layers and finally my net.

My right arm was feeling the effects of a good half-hour battle and when I lifted it out of the water onto my waiting mat in the boat I just knew I had something special.

Back on the island, and my Reubens span round to 45½lb, new p.b. and elated so I sacked him up in the deep margins to my right, the old lake record carp had put on some weight. Over the next ten to fifteen minutes my phone bill shot up as I phoned a few people to see who was available to take some photos.

I was just sorting out the rod that I'd caught with when one of my two left-handers bleeped twice. I looked at the rod, but nothing moved. I suspected a crafty carp shaking his or her head so picked up the rod and struck in the hope that I was right. I could hardly believe it, I was in again, the rod bending nicely with me forced to give line as it steamed off, obviously very unhappy at being hooked. Once again I donned my life jacket and pushed the boat out to take up battle once more. As I made my way towards the hooked carp I could once again sense that it was a lump, as it stayed deep.

The fight was just as awesome as the previous battle and once again it wasn't until nearly fifteen minutes had passed that I saw the carp clearly enough to identify it. It was 'big scaly' and she looked just that, big!

Knowing what was on the other end just made the next few minutes an incredible awesome experience. My right arm, tired from the first fight, was feeling the effects and 'big scaly' certainly didn't want to give up and used all her weight to gain depth and distance no sooner had I gained some line. I looked at my watch and it showed I'd been in the boat twenty-five minutes before she began to tire. As I slowly pulled her closer and closer somehow I just knew my time had come, and

What a fish... I was lucky enough to witness both of Martin Clarke's whackers, this 45½lb heavily plated mirror and an even bigger mirror of 46lb 2oz.

when she finally kissed the spreader block I was buzzing big style.

I find it immensely difficult to describe the sense of achievement I felt in catching these particular carp, so glad my time had come. I bit my main line and hoisted her aboard to lie gently on the mat in the boat. As I lifted her I realized she was bigger than I expected, bloody hell what will she weigh!

Full monty back to my swim on the island and then I put her back in the water still in the net. Luckily I had two sacks tucked away so after wetting the other sack I got her out onto the unhooking mat to get the hook out, eliminator rig doing the buzz. She looked massive and once I carried her to my scales hanging from a nearby tree I soon found out just how big. As I slowly let the scales take the strain the needle shot past 30lb then 40lb to rest finally at 46lb 2oz. I was gobsmacked; surely I must be dreaming so I double-checked. I sacked her up next to the other sack and put the kettle on before rolling a smoke.

I pondered on whether to tell anyone or not before they turned up, in the end I reached for my mobile and said more camera film may be required. Two personal bests, one after the other, and two lake records on the trot too! I reeled my other two rods in and packed them all away, for some reason I just couldn't bring myself to carry on fishing.

By now Martin Clarke, a pretty fit bloke, it has to be said, was knackered. It was hardly surprising: he had just experienced a unique moment in carp fishing, one few will ever realize. And so, after the fish were photographed and gently released, the few who had gathered to witness the event slowly dissipated. It's funny the traffic was far less of a problem on the way back home.

That evening I pondered on the catch. The combined weight of the brace – 91lb 10oz – landed in less than an hour was remarkable, especially when I looked back through the archives. Just short of thirty years before, John Macleod landed the then largest brace of carp in a single sitting. His Redmire Pool catch of 1972 weighed in at 68½lb, the fish being recorded individually at 40lb and 28½lb.

But oh, how things change in a comparatively short time frame! There have of course been other amazing brace captures that I've marvelled at, but none as graphic as Martin's Summerleaze brace. I only wish more people could have seen these fish in the flesh.

Many of the stock of Summerleaze carp have been caught over the years; indeed I have individually photographed both Martin's fish in the past, but nowhere near the size they were on his special day. Indeed, it was not long ago that Kevin Dean furnished me with pictures from many moons ago, one of the fish being the fully scaled one at 28½lb from September 1994 plus another caught by a lad in the late 1970s which I can't identify.

The Sandy Fish

However, all the fish mentioned are put in the shade by an infamous Summerleaze carp known as the Sandy Fish. This carp has been repeatedly seen by a wide variety of Summerleaze anglers, including Martin Clarke.

Without doubt the best story I have about this fish concerns Ian Russell. It was another time when I went to the lake to take photographs of a big (over 40lb) carp that Ian had caught. He fished long and hard at the lake, catching a few of its prized occupants. But it was his story of the Sandy fish that captured my imagination the most.

On this particular visit, after the pictures had been taken, Ian proceeded to tell me about a very large carp called the Sandy one. 'It's a funny thing,' he started, "But the only time I've seen it, it's always had the only bream in the place alongside. The bream is a big'un, gotta be over ten pounds,' he concluded. 'When someone's going to put this carp on the bank, it's got to feed at some stage on angler's baits,' I asked. 'You're right, Chris,' continued Ian, 'but so far it's not made a mistake."

Perhaps, I thought, it might make a mistake with one of Ian's baits tonight? On the way back home and just 20 minutes into the trip, no traffic to speak of, my mobile phone rang. 'It's Ian, Ian Russell.' I screeched to a halt. 'What, Ian?' I shouted out. 'What have you done?' 'I nearly caught the Sandy Fish,' he retorted, half-laughing down the phone. 'How come?' I enquired.

Denys Watkins-Pitchford, 'BB', whose writings of fishing for carp dating from after the Second World War inspired so many when carp fishing was in its infancy. This grand old gentleman is seen here with two of the first purpose-built hand-made Richard Walker split-cane carp rods from the very early 1950s.

It transpired that his first cast back into the swim produced a run in short order … and in came the bream! It was a big'un at over ten pounds, just like he'd told me. Who knows, Ian Russell could have been just one bait away from the famed Sandy Fish – how exciting is that!

Time marches on, and though fish have died at Summerleaze in recent times, there are still big carp to be found in its clear, weedy depths. Its fame as a big fish venue has been founded on the anglers who fished there and of course the carp themselves – they will always be known, to me anyway, as Summerleaze stunners.

SUMMARY

From the beginnings of the deliberate pursuit of catching carp with rod and line right up to the present day, no other fish evokes the same emotions, obsession and almost dream-like qualities that fishing for carp can bring to an angler. Of course the size of the beasties, their cunning (when they grow big) and their almost universal presence in all kinds of habitat give us the situation we find now in 2006 – carp is by far the most popular freshwater fish to catch in this country.

With that said, let me end with this thought. In terms of significance, no other carp water in this country has the pedigree or longevity of Redmire Pool. Its importance as a breeding ground for new ideas in carp fishing, be it rods, reels, line, terminal tackle, tactics, baits and much more, cannot be overstated. The fact that it once held the largest (three consecutive record fish spanning almost thirty years) carp in the land in its depths meant it often attracted the best carp anglers. They strove over the years to come to terms with their quarry, and in the process we have all benefited by new and improved techniques.

Let us also not forget the magic of fishing at Redmire itself. Denys Watkins-Pitchford, better known as 'BB', wrote in his delightful little book, *Wood Pool* (Putnam, 1958 and republished by Medlar Press in the 1990s), 'At Redmire there is always the consoling thought that you may be suddenly taken by a really fabulous fish. I have seen at least one there which was like a bronze row boat. I hesitate to estimate its weight, but I certainly put it at over 50lb.

'These creatures seemed to me, in the hours of darkness, as fish not of this earth. They are at least prehistoric monsters.'

3. My Quest for Carp

by Tony Gibson

HUMBLE BEGINNINGS

When I was first asked to contribute to this book, I asked what it was that I was being asked specifically to write about. The answer I got at first appeared to be good news, as I was given a fairly free format and was simply asked to write about my own progression through the various stages in my carp fishing 'career'. Later though, as I thought about it some more, I had some misgivings, as it can be difficult to write something of interest when there is no specific theme or message that needs to be put across to the reader. However, as I started to consider how the various waters and associated fish that I've targeted have changed over time and how my approach and associated tackle and bait have developed alongside the various challenges that have been presented, I came to realize that maybe there is something to be learnt from my own experiences. I also realized that as I'm not a 'carp only' specialist (I like to ring the changes between most of our regular coarse fish species), the time that I actually spend carp fishing probably has more in common with the more typical carp fisherman than with the more dedicated carp specialist (who would perhaps be a more likely contributor to a carp-only publication of this nature).

So we'll get stuck in and take a ramble through the various places and events throughout my fishing lifetime that have been associated with trying to put the odd carp on the bank, and see how we get on. A good place to start will be at the beginning …

When I was much younger, the first few carp that I caught were more by accident than design and were not of a weight that would interest the majority of the carp fishermen reading this book, so we'll not waste any time in recounting these particular events. In my youth I did actually spend a bit of time trying to catch one of the odd carp that had found their way into my local park nature trail lake, but these early efforts tended to be of a rather opportunist nature, usually when I was ill equipped for the task and tended to end in failure rather than success … so perhaps it's best we skip over these events as well.

When I finally decided to catch some decent carp by design, I selected a day-ticket water not too far from home that teemed with carp from very small to just into double figures. The water in question would probably come under the 'carp puddle' classification nowadays, but back then these weren't really popular and the classification didn't exist. The numbers of carp had by all accounts been created by accident, when the owner discovered that the breeding conditions suited the carp that he'd stocked so well that the water was occasionally netted in order to reduce the total fish biomass slightly and give

Early success on a home-made bait appears to have stunned me into a coma.

some of the other species a chance to grow. The owner did actually run a carp syndicate water nearby, but due to my lack of funds and reliable transport arrangements (I was still at school at the time) for my early experiments I concentrated on trying to catch the bigger carp from the 'mixed' fishery.

I had already read with interest the carp-related articles that appeared in the monthly magazines of the time and had also borrowed a copy of Jim Gibbinson's *Carp* book, which had been published some time earlier. I was also starting to get interested in the application of carp-related tackle, tactics and bait to tench fishing, so I had done some groundwork already. I had a basic understanding of some of the end-tackle arrangements, and the hair-rig had also recently been published in Kevin

Maddocks' *Carp Fever*, with variations on the theme already appearing in the occasional magazine article. Also around this time, I spent plenty of time in the kitchen messing around with various carp bait and boilie ingredients, flavours and attractors, some sourced at great expense from the few carp bait suppliers that had started to appear at the time and others from chemists and supermarkets. I also had the advantage of being able to quiz my dad (a former analytical chemist and a science teacher at the time) about some of the theories and science behind the bait-related writings, some of which were pretty heavy-going.

I should perhaps make it clear at this point that at the time of the experiments I am describing here, a ready-made boilie of any type had yet to appear on the market.

83

A couple of fish that got the 'monkeys' flying.

Most people put together their own mixes if a paste or boilie bait was required, all boilies being rolled by hand, as, again, commercially available rolling equipment had yet to hit the tackle shops.

It was interesting to note that some of the suggested carp boilie recipes appearing in print at the time proved to be almost, if not totally, impossible to roll into balls that stayed together. Some would never really bind together and would fall apart during the tedious hand-rolling process while other recipes tended to break apart either during or following the boiling stage. I'm convinced that some of these recipes were put together more in the author's mind than in a mixing bowl, and that some had never been tested in a true fishing scenario before being committed to print.

My initial intention was to create a bait and presentation that would deter the attentions of the hundreds of smaller carp and other species in the venue, but still prove attractive and acceptable to the 'big' ones.

My bait ended up being a concoction based on a readily available milk protein powder (Casilan) sourced from the local chemist, and other ingredients and binders available through specialist carp bait mail-order outlets. Only a single 10 or 12oz mix was made up in the kitchen at any one time, because, as I've already mentioned, the baits had to be painstakingly hand-rolled prior to boiling. I actually got quite proficient at this and even managed to perfect the technique of rolling two boilies at a time, but the task still seemed to take forever.

The chosen rig was a simple running ledger with a nylon hook link, with a hair made from a much finer nylon line tied to the eye and fixed to the shank of the hook, just where the bend of the hook starts, with a small section of thin-bore rig tube. Bite indication was by means of an original and unconverted Optonic bite alarm and home-made 'monkey climber'. The needle of the monkey climber was made from a fibreglass quiver tip blank cut to the required length while the 'monkey' was made from a white wine bottle cap with the closed end cut off so it could slip over the needle with a section cut out of the side to retain the mainline between reel and alarm. It was fortunate that the wine bottle caps were cheap enough to buy in bulk and simple enough to convert into monkeys, as runs inevitably resulted in the monkey flying off in any old direction, occasionally never to be seen again. It proved unrealistic to try and tether the monkey with line, thread or anything else, as tangles could well occur, and a ready supply of pre-cut monkeys kept somewhere near the rod was a good idea if a hectic session was expected.

The use of two rods was allowed at the venue but I had too much fun float fishing with bread to give up both rods to the new specialist approach, so I fished only one rod with the boilie and hair-rig approach.

No pre-baiting was necessary as the carp took to the new bait from the very first trip. Indeed, results were encouraging, as every trip out resulted in a number of carp and the occasional tench falling to the rod fishing the new approach. The trips were only day trips and the fish only singles, but the important thing was that I was enjoying myself and constantly learning through actually catching fish.

Not big by today's standards, but back then a fish like this was still a prize to me.

Once I'd satisfied myself that I had a bait and method that would catch, I took the opportunity to play around and experiment with various bait ingredients and tactics. Doing this increased the learning curve and also taught me that not everything written about carp and carp fishing can be applied to the waters you are fishing and the carp you are trying to catch. Every water is unique and will require a unique approach to get the best results.

RESERVOIR CARPING

I was keen to get a few double-figure carp under my belt and was also looking for a well-stocked carp water to give me plenty of scope to continue experimenting with rigs and bait.

Therefore it wasn't a difficult decision to join the syndicate being run on a local reservoir when the chance came my way. This particular water was around fifty-five acres and well stocked with stacks of carp in the single and double figure bracket, with the outside chance of a fish over the twenty-pound mark. The reservoir also contained some catfish, and at the time this wasn't a species I'd ever encountered before, so it was extra icing on the cake.

From a carping perspective, this particular water gave me a great opportunity to learn the reactions of the fish to a range of baits and rigs and to try out a number of ideas. At this stage in my carping development I thought that it would be great to try out a range of different rigs and methods and to have the chance to try out and gain confidence with some of my own theories and ideas.

It is all very well plugging away at the sparsely stocked, difficult big-fish waters, where a run once in a blue flash is all that can be hoped for. The trouble is these types of waters don't really give you much of a

chance to experiment, let alone gain confidence with unfamiliar baits or methods. Unless you can see the reaction of the carp, the hard waters give you very little feedback. A well-stocked runs water, on the other hand, suits the bill for that sort of thing quite nicely.

Baiting Experiments

Once I'd got my ticket for the reservoir sorted out I did a couple of overnight sessions on the narrow, shallower end. This produced a few carp, including a double or two, so with these fish under my belt, I was eager to start experimenting. The first trials I wanted to carry out on the reservoir carp were to do with bait. First of all I wanted to make a comparison between a particle approach and a purely boilie baiting scenario. The next overnighter in a new swim further towards the dam end of the reservoir was based around a particle approach, with a couple of pints of maples catapulted as far out into the swim as possible and double maple hookbaits fished on both rods. After a fish, or a lengthy period of inactivity, I would fire out a further few pouchfuls of maples into the swim. This certainly led to quite a busy session with several fish, including a couple of low doubles, coming to the landing net from late evening until I packed up later the following morning.

The following week I was back in the same swim for another Friday night overnight session, but this time with boilies as bait and not a particle in sight. To ensure the difference in the two baiting approaches were marked, I only used reasonably large 18mm boilies for the session. Once again the catapult was put to work in order to fire out around 100 baits into the general area to be fished and the same boilies were used as hook baits and cast out amongst the free offerings. Again

Fishing alone, I just took a quick photograph of this mirror carp.

the results were encouraging and a number of fish were landed. The major difference between this session and the week before was the average size of the fish. This time the fish averaged around 2lb more than in the previous session, and included a couple more doubles.

My bait experiments continued over a number of following sessions. I was also able to compare results with a friend who had also joined the water, and once I'd got to know some of the regulars I was in a position to share information and compare notes with some of the other carpers on the water.

It soon became apparent that particles produced plenty of fish, so if you were after runs and on a limited bait budget, then this was the way to go. Boilies tended to produce fewer fish, but the average size was better and the bigger fish in the water nearly always fell to a boilie fished in one way or another.

What was perhaps more interesting was that results started to indicate that different boilies produced different results. Boilie recipes with what could be termed a low food-value base and made up using a relatively high synthetic flavour level appeared to produce similar results to particle baits and produced lots of fish, but the average size tended to be smaller. However, boilies based on a much better food value base and containing only low flavour levels, or no flavour at all, and made up with a liquid food content (such as Multimino) still produced reasonable numbers of fish, but with a noticeably higher average size.

These results were certainly no fluke or coincidence – comparative results could be guessed at the start of a session and then measured and confirmed session after session. The knowledge that the boilies based on a relatively sound nutritional base and only natural and/or very low flavour level attractors helped catch carp of a bigger

Set up on the reservoir, ready for the next run, in the summer of 1989.

than average size is still central to my approach to carp fishing today.

Backleads

Another valuable lesson that I learned at the reservoir concerned the use of backleads. Admittedly, I rarely have the opportunity to use backleads nowadays, as I do not like to use them in weedy waters unless I'm fishing very close to the bank. However, on the reservoir they were an absolute godsend.

With the obvious exception of the dam area, much of the reservoir's contours remained relatively featureless in terms of depth variation; essentially, the water very gradually deepened the further out you went from the margins. This meant that in most areas the margins were very shallow, and in fact the water remained so even quite a way out. This could often lead to problems, with plenty of potential tangles when playing and landing fish. I certainly had a few moments myself with rods being passed over and under each other all too often during some of the lengthy scraps that the mad commons especially liked to subject you to. I was also witness to some absolute beauties where a fine mainline knitting job had been done by a particularly inventive fish tearing around someone's swim! For some, the initial sweet sound of the buzzer sounding off all too often turned into a living nightmare, as a tangle of epic proportions resulted.

Fortunately I managed to retain my sanity as I soon discovered the benefit of light backleads that could easily be clipped onto the line after casting out and simply plopped into the water in front of the appropriate rod tip. This made a huge difference as it nearly always kept the mainline on the inactive rod/rods out of harm's way while a fish was being played on another rod. The backlead certainly didn't appear to make any appreciable difference to bite detection, and the vast majority of the takes were absolute 'fliers' anyway!

It would be difficult to conclude that the number of takes increased due to backleading; the difference certainly wouldn't have been terribly significant. However, it's not hard to believe that the carp were that bit more comfortable in the swim because the backleads helped to keep the mainline pinned down all the way from the rod tip to the baited end tackle.

What also made me happy to use the backleads was the fact that the lake bed hardly contained any weed whatsoever. In fact finding a strand draped over the lead when marking the swim was an event of major significance! Therefore the backlead sliding about on the mainline and keeping the mainline near the fish relatively close to the bottom during a fight didn't pose any extra threat of getting snagged up. In weedy waters, where a backlead could cause problems if it got stuck up in weed

One of many days when things were going right at the reservoir.

when playing a fish, I'm very loth to use them. In fact, I'd only use them in a situation where I was convinced that the lead could be easily ejected if it did snag up – and use of a backlead was likely to significantly increase my chances of a take in the first instance.

Floater Fishing

Another aspect of the fishing at the reservoir that provided plenty of interesting action was the floater fishing opportunities. During the right conditions, the reservoir carp could be really switched on to the floaters, and fast and furious action could be had if you got the baiting and methods nicely sorted out. At certain times during periods of warm weather, the carp would shoal up and mill around close to the surface in large groups. These were opportunities not to be missed, and although fishing with baits presented on the bottom was still a viable proposition at these times, the amount of action didn't come anywhere near what could be achieved with floating baits. Besides which, floater fishing was an awful lot of fun and watching the carp's reaction to the floaters and all that close-range visual 'will it, won't it have it?' type stuff is exciting and rather addictive.

Whenever I turned up for a session and found the carp in the right mood for the floaters, I'd grab a big bag of mixers (that were always kept in the back of the car) together with a couple of catapults, and start firing out freebies. I'd keep up the flow of freebies using a little and often principle while setting up a simple floater outfit with a medium-sized controller and a long floating hooklink of around 8lb breaking strain terminating in a size 10 hook. This initial feeding period was important to the overall success of the venture, and the more time spent initially feeding the surface-feeding shoals with the freebie mixers, the better the overall results. Continuing to feed the carp with the free offerings without putting out a hookbait encouraged the fish to continue feeding and look out for more without becoming suspicious. Obviously sooner or later the temptation to catch one of the hordes of fish gulping down the mixers would become too great and after checking that the landing net was made up and in a handy position, a cast with a mixer glued to the hook would have to be made. So long as sufficient time had been taken to whip the carp up into a feeding frenzy, a take on the hookbait was never long in coming.

Once you'd started catching, it was important not to get carried away in all of the excitement and to ensure that a steady stream of the loose mixers were available to the carp still milling around out in the swim. Developing a certain rhythm and constantly topping up the free mixers floating around the swim would help to allay the suspicions of the fish in front of you and would also encourage any passing fish to join in the feeding spell. What I'd do was to continue feeding in the freebies while setting up the other rods, bivvy or whatever. Once it looked as though the fish were back into a confident feeding mode, I'd then make another cast with the floater gear and help myself to another fish.

If I could instil in myself the necessary discipline to keep the feed topped up and not plunder the swim too early, or over too long a period, the feeding could be stretched out for the remaining daylight hours, with a seemingly never-ending supply of feeding carp coming into the swim, and the odd fish caught on the floater gear at intervals throughout the day. A very impressive number of fish could therefore be caught in total, with a better end result than if the swim had been fished out in the early stages.

NEXT STEP:
A GRAVEL PIT

Soon enough I got the urge to fish a proper gravel pit. A vast amount of the more influential and technical books and articles dedicated to carp fishing at the time were written primarily by anglers fishing and catching from gravel pits, most of which were in the southern half of the country.

Anglers such as Rod Hutchinson, Kevin Maddocks and Jim Gibbinson, to name but a few, were very influential in formulating ideas around baits and methods, and these anglers appeared to primarily be practising their art in the pits in the Colne Valley, Kent and elsewhere.

At the time it was all too easy to be swept up in the excitement of all the new developments and baits that were being talked and written about, and I was keen to try out some carp fishing on a fully fledged gravel pit for myself.

Looking around the waters that were available reasonably close to home, I came up with a number of potential candidates. I investigated a handful and fished the odd few on occasion. However, there was one Cambridgeshire pit in particular that really grabbed my attention and it held a magical fascination for me for more than two years.

The details of the pit were originally obtained from what used to be the old Amy Roadstone Company (ARC) fisheries booklet that came with membership of the ARC Angling Association. I'd originally joined ARC AA for the non-carp-related fishing available on their Thrapston Lagoon fishery, a very large gravel pit in the Nene Valley in Northamptonshire. However, it was this other gravel pit in the Ouse Valley, between Huntington and Cambridge, and virtually unknown within carp circles at the time, that appeared to fit the bill in terms of what I was looking for

from a carp-fishing perspective. The pit was called Fen Drayton.

Challenges at Fen Drayton

Looking back, I was perhaps ill-prepared to tackle such a demanding venue. However, there is nothing to beat a hefty dose of enthusiasm, and I was certainly fired up after my first look round during the close season.

Once the new season was underway and I'd fished my first few sessions on the water, it soon became apparent that the rumours of there being very few carp to have a go at were not very far from the truth. I'd yet to receive any action on the rods, apart from eels, which were to prove quite a menace, but more importantly I'd yet to see any carp in the water. I was doing all the textbook things like fishing into the wind and spending quite a bit of time looking around, but fish were proving impossible to locate.

Most of the entertainment came from the windsurfers, who were very active during the day at weekends. The antics of some of the unfortunate beginners who would inevitably get blown down to the windward end of the water and then be unable to get back to base often provided a few laughs. The frequent irritation of a wetsuited novice falling off their board countless times over your baited areas was more than compensated for when one of the more shapely lady beginners needed rescuing from the margins after becoming stranded. Without the necessary skills to get herself back towards her starting point and having fallen from her board countless times, she eventually found herself exhausted and unable to extract herself from my swim. She was very apologetic as I helped to drag both her and her windsurfing board onto dry land, but was soon feeling more comfortable as she relaxed by the

Sunset on a big water: the view from my bivvy.

bivvy, drying her long blonde hair with a towel from my kit bag and warming herself up with a cup of tea that I'd quickly put together. However, for some strange reason her boyfriend appeared less than impressed when he eventually came round to see us over an hour later to find out what had happened after she'd disappeared from view!

Eels

The consistent eel activity on the baits that I'd originally decided to try on Fen Drayton led to my first tactical change.

I'd originally decided to try two different baits on the Fen Drayton carp to see what happened. The first choice was home-made boilies based on what could probably be termed as mid-protein base mix. I reckoned that not only would this be an attractive base in its own right, but it could also be a useful base for any attractors and/or flavours that I might want to experiment with. The other bait I wanted to use was either paste or lightly skinned boilies made from Rod Hutchinson's 'Seafood Blend' base mix with no other attractors or flavours added to what came out of the packet. The 'Seafood Blend' was a mix that I'd enjoyed some success with on the tench from a large Midlands reservoir the previous season. Its effectiveness with the tench and the positive reports I'd received from other anglers gave me plenty of confidence in this particular bait. The added convenience of being able to very quickly knock up some paste by simply mixing some base mix with lake water further enhanced its appeal.

Unfortunately both these baits quickly proved to be highly attractive to the pit's eel population. In fact, one of the first eels caught early on the very first night I ever spent on the water stood as a personal best for a number of years.

Most nights fishing with the original choice of baits would result in at least an eel or two having to be unceremoniously hauled on to the bank. This was not much to my liking for a couple of major reasons. Firstly, I felt that I couldn't get the pit's population of carp used to finding my bait, nor gauge how much bait was in a swim at any one time, because I felt that most of the time it was being eaten by the eels within a relatively short space of time. Secondly, I didn't much like having to handle them when I caught one. Nowadays I'm much more comfortable about handling and unhooking eels, thanks to learning the simple procedure of laying the eels on their backs and waiting for them to stop squirming about before dealing with them. During my early Fen Drayton days, however, landing eels meant being prepared for a slimy wrestling match that often went hand-in-hand with the total destruction of a lovingly tied and carefully tuned end tackle.

In order to overcome the eel problems, I was tempted to switch over completely to a particle approach. However, at the time I wasn't comfortable fishing particles at range and felt that relying solely on particles would be too limiting. Fortunately, just in the nick of time, Nutrabaits brought out a nutritional birdseed-based boilie mix called Ener-vite that seemed to be just the thing I was looking for. From what I'd read, it seemed as though Ener-vite would

When a big fish gets caught it's handy if there is the odd pair of helping hands for the weighing and photo rituals.

not prove terribly attractive to the eels and could be complemented by the use of a carefully chosen essential oil as an attractor. Geranium oil had something of a track record so I decided to use that, with molasses syrup in the Ener-vite as a natural sweetener and to help darken the bait to make it look less conspicuous.

Once I'd started using the Ener-vite, the problems with the eels disappeared. This was great, and eventually my baiting strategy became based entirely on this boilie mix with the aforementioned liquid ingredients.

My first summer on Fen was frustrating for a number of reasons. Working in London and not driving or owning a car at the time meant that simply getting to and from the venue was a struggle, with me having to rely totally on lifts from my girl-friend or any mates I could persuade to join me. Then the eels had been a nuisance and I'd not sorted out a bait I was happy with until it was late on in the year. Plus there was the fact that I'd seen very little carp activity and had almost no one to compare notes with, as although the odd carper showed up to fish the place on occasions, nobody other than me appeared to be prepared to stick with the place.

As the summer months started to turn to winter, I decided to leave Fen until the following season. That was until a couple of weeks before Christmas, when I suddenly decided that part of the reason behind my lack of success could have been that my baits were competing with a stack of natural food and that I may have a better chance now that the water was colder and a large proportion of the natural food stocks had died off.

Winter Fishing

My chosen swim for this first winter overnight session on Fen was one that had recently been created from some minor back-filling after some more gravel pits had been dug in the vicinity. This had turned a corner of the pit into dry land and had given access to a couple of features that had previously been out of casting range. As this area was also receiving the full force of a very stiff north-westerly blow that was adding a fair bit of colour to the margins, I thought this was as good a place as any to pitch up.

I arrived late in the afternoon and really had to rush around in order to get a couple of baits and some freebies out towards the features. The strong winds blowing into my face did nothing to aid casting and baiting up, and I ended up falling a little short of the feature I'd wanted to fish to. It was virtually dark by the time I got round

to dropping in a third bait close to the stirred-up margins to my left, and it was totally dark by the time I was able to start erecting the bivvy and putting together the bits and bobs that make life on the bank a little more comfortable.

Actually getting the bivvy together was something of a major chore, especially as I wanted the bivvy close to and facing the rods. In those days commercially available remote systems for the bite alarms weren't around, and I needed to be sure I'd hear an alarm over the noise from the wind and the waves crashing into the bank if I was to be fortunate enough to get a bite. Also, back then the choice of bankside living accommodation wasn't great and I was making do with a large fishing umbrella and nylon 'overwrap' to turn it into a bivvy setup. This type of arrangement wasn't too bad to erect in only a light breeze or with the wind coming from behind. When facing the teeth of a near gale, and on ground that was very loose due to being made up of recently dug-up and deposited material, however, made things nearly impossible. I almost lost the entire set-up on a couple of occasions while trying to throw the over-wrap over the umbrella that was shoved into the ground, and at one stage had to go racing after the umbrella after it had blown out of the ground. After having retrieved and folded up the umbrella I then had to go off into the dark again to find the over-wrap that had blown away in the mean-time, eventually having to climb a tree in order to retrieve it after it had got stuck halfway up. Eventually, after what seemed the best part of an entire lifetime, I managed to get the bivvy put together and the bedchair, sleeping bag and cooking equipment out.

Getting some sleep that night proved difficult. The gusting wind ensured that the buzzers gave off the odd bleep every now and again no matter how I set the rods up,

A calm and peaceful morning on Fen Drayton in June 1991.

and also caused an irritating amount of flapping of the bivvy sides, especially as the pegs at the front were constantly working loose in the loose earth. In the end I used a number of spare banksticks to replace the front pegs, as these could be forced a long way into the ground and didn't work loose as quickly.

Eventually I did fall asleep, but whatever had gone on the previous evening and night had not prepared me for the scene that greeted me the following morning. Although the wind had calmed down in relative terms from the previous day, its reconstructive effect on the swim was quite dramatic to say the least! The battering of the waves on the loose earth that made up the area of my swim had caused an impressive amount of bankside erosion overnight. The dry land at the front of the swim where I'd put the rod rests in was now covered by at least a foot of water. The buzzers themselves were either at or just above the actual waterline, and it was only the fact that I'd used the longest banksticks I had and had forced them as far into the ground

as I possibly could that had prevented them from collapsing. The bivvy itself didn't look to be in much better shape and was sitting almost entirely in water as the topsoil had been washed away. The banksticks that I'd used to peg the front of the bivvy down were now mostly waving around in gravel that was itself covered by several inches of water, and there were even a couple of inches of water around the front legs of the bedchair. My stove, boots, bait bag and rucksack were sitting in water and it was only the carryall that I used to cart my sleeping bag and food provisions around in that was still left on dry land right at the back of the bivvy. It wasn't a pleasant surprise at that time on a cold December morning, and having to wade around in cold water to retrieve all the gear and set things up on firm dry land again was not a pleasurable experience.

At least one of the buzzers never recovered from the experience and I must have been affected quite a bit myself, as any further plans for winter carp fishing trips to Fen Drayton were quickly forgotten.

Second Season

The following season nearly started in disaster before it had even begun. I'd finished working in London and had sorted out my own transport, an old but spacious and comfortable Renault estate. I'd loaded the motor up with enough tackle, bait and provisions to cover a three-day session and arrived at Fen Drayton soon after first light on the morning of the 15 June, eager to start looking round for signs of carp activity before finding somewhere to pitch in anticipation of the start of the season.

So I got a nasty shock when I discovered new signs dotted around the place showing that the ownership of the fishing rights had changed hands and that now a local club controlled the fishing. There were no contact numbers on the notices, so I had no clue as to how to go about obtaining the correct ticket, or whatever, to enable me to fish. As it was still early morning, I did a circuit of the lake, looking for signs of fish before deciding to head into the village and ask someone if they knew about the local fishing club. One of the first persons I bumped into was the local postman doing his rounds. He directed me to the local post office, where he was sure I'd be able to obtain some information. Unfortunately this proved not to be the case, so with little else to go on I headed back to the pit, hoping I would come across another angler to quiz about the new arrangements. As luck would have it, I soon came across the old ARC bailiff, a bit of a character called 'Jug' (it was the ears). Anyway, it transpired that Jug was now the bailiff for the club that had taken on the fishing rights and could issue me with the required ticket that morning – sorted!

This season things seemed to click into place a lot easier. Moving jobs and having my own transport helped enormously, as I could spend a bit more time at the water and also come and go at times more to my choosing rather than fit around other people's schedules. Perhaps by becoming more familiar with the water, I also seemed to be seeing a few fish on a more regular basis.

With all this, and the fact that with the Ener-vite I'd now got a bait that the carp would like but eels would pretty much leave alone, my confidence started to increase and I felt I was getting closer to putting one of the pit's elusive carp on the bank.

Then, the following month, it finally happened.

I had started concentrating on a nicely featured swim on the south bank. Previously I'd been shying away from this bank as it was rarely on the receiving end of the wind and I'd been doing all the regular textbook stuff like fishing into the wind. However, now I was seeing a few fish it appeared that on Fen Drayton, for whatever reason, this made little difference and the fish seemed to turn up wherever they liked despite the wind direction. The fancied swim had several gravel bars and humps within reasonable casting range and a deep gully running close to the bank. The swim also had some previous form. Learning that I'd started carping on Fen Drayton, a friend had dabbled with the venue the previous season, concentrating on the easy-to-access south bank, and eventually landing a fine looking 28-pounder for his efforts!

Looking forward to a two-night session, I'd arrived late in the afternoon and quickly set about getting three rods out to the chosen areas. If the sun was right, and with the aid of a decent pair of polaroids, you could often see the major bars from the high bank. However, I still used a marker float to be sure of getting the rods onto the clear areas and to help ensure that the free offerings were catapulted out accurately around the hookbaits. I was using

18mm baits which were reasonably heavy and catapulted out a good way. I preferred a catapult to a throwing stick in these situations where I was fishing all three baits on different features, as I tend to be more accurate with a catapult than a throwing stick.

Hookbaits were 18mm pop-ups made from moulding regular boilie paste around suitably sized cork balls prior to boiling, and they were mounted on to long-shank size 6 fly hooks bent into the bent-hook pattern that was starting to make all the news in the carp media at the time.

The middle and right-hand rod were fished to shallow gravel features between thirty-five and fifty yards out, while the left-hand rod was fished towards the base of the marginal shelf as it sloped off to form the near edge of the gully.

With the rods out and supper made, I could relax on the bedchair and look out of the bivvy doorway for any carpy-looking signs, and amuse myself with the antics of the family of field mice that had started to become used to the regular weekly appearance of my bivvy and would gather at the doorway waiting for it to get dark before rummaging around looking for crumbs and odd baits.

As I started to relax and soak up the atmosphere of my surroundings, I was suddenly brought to attention by a beep from the Optonic on the middle rod. A series of several beeps saw the indicator creeping up to the top of the needle and me standing by the rod ready to strike. It turned out to be a liner, however, as once the line got tight with the indicator at the top of the needle, it suddenly fell slack and the indicator dropped back to its original position. Two minutes later the same thing happened again. There were obviously fish in the swim. A short while later the alarm on the

The 29lb 8oz carp from Fen Drayton.

Back she goes.

Most of the night was quiet and uneventful – that was, up until around 3.30am, when it appeared that the bream had come back on a return journey as the liners started again. This time it was the right-hand rod that indicated the first line bite, with several separate indications of fish movement before the middle rod joined in. Again, the left-hand rod fishing close in was silent, obviously missing out as the shoal moved around further out from the bank. As had happened the previous evening, the liners lasted for over an hour before tailing off and leaving peace and quiet as the new morning sun crept over the trees on the horizon. After the early wake-up call from the bream shoal liners, I was still rather sleepy and lay propped up on one elbow, half in and half out of the sleeping bag watching the calm surface of the water in front of the swim.

A single beep from the middle rod had me wondering whether the bream were making a return when suddenly everything pulled up tight and the Bait Runner and alarm sounded out in unison as something tore off with the bait. In a flash I was up with the rod in my hand, bending into the fish before it belted off too far over the back of the bars.

The fight was steady and without any major hiccups, with the fish behaving itself and managing to stay clear of any snags and the other lines. Before too long it was in the net and I was able to have a quick peek before making it secure and sorting out the unhooking and weighing gear. It was an obvious PB and first 20lb+ carp, with the scales finally recording a weight of 29lb 8oz. All the hard work and effort from the previous season, and the pulling together of the pieces of the jigsaw had finally come good and I was overjoyed with the result. Perhaps not a monster on a national scale, but to me it was a terrific achievement and a proud, unforgettable moment.

right-hand rod started with the odd bleep and soon enough the alarms on both rods were rarely silent as fish after fish brushed against the lines.

I guessed it must have been a bream shoal that was causing all the activity. It seemed as if it was far too much fish movement to have been caused by the carp. In fact, the almost constant liners kept up for around an hour and a half before stopping as suddenly as they'd begun.

ELSTOW

The reservoir carp provided plenty of action, and it was a very useful place to try out baits and rigs. Fen Drayton was a challenging water, full of mystery, and had taught me a number of useful lessons. However, now I was on the look-out for a new water to carp fish. I was after something less physically demanding (and less of a 'head banger') than Fen, but with a proven track record and preferably a few thirties to have a go for. Fortunately I'd been planning ahead and had got myself on the waiting list for the syndicate of a rather useful sounding clay pit near Bedford called Elstow.

Actually there are two pits on the complex and obviously a lot of thought had gone into the naming of the waters, as they were commonly known as Pit 1 and Pit 2. Pit 1 was the water I was most interested in as it sounded like you could expect at least a few runs per season, rather than Pit 2, which only had a dozen or so fish and a tough reputation.

The year I gained membership I had to do a work party in the close season. This was all inspiring stuff as it was a hot sunny

Elstow potential: another Pit 1 thirty.

A mid-thirty from Elstow 1, this one called 'the Unattended'.

day in late May and the carp were very much in evidence, cruising around in the upper layers, letting everyone have a good look at them. It was great to be able to see virtually all of the water's carp on display, although my estimates of the weights of the fish appeared to be a little low for the size of the fish that I'd been led to believe were in residence.

I had lunch and a cold beer in a local pub before heading back to the lake for final work party duties followed by another slow walk around the lake. This later look round was a bit of an eye-opener, as most of the residential carp were still on display, but this time it appeared that a far greater number of big fish were to be seen. Obviously the carp that I'd seen earlier in the day hadn't somehow been replaced with fish several pounds bigger. What had happened was that as the day progressed and the sun had moved round in the sky, the optical perspective on the fish was changed; essentially, the fish had simply appeared smaller during the early observations than they did later on in the day.

This was a valuable lesson learned, and now I'm always careful not to be too precise about putting weights to fish that I'm looking at in the water unless I've got a definite reference, such as a known fish at a known weight, to compare the other fish with.

Carpers plugged into the carp-fishing grapevine were well aware of the potential of Elstow Pit 1 and the water was a busy syndicate, fished by a number of very capable carp anglers. Some of the members were full-time during the more productive months of the year and fished the venue as often as the syndicate rotation system and rules would allow. This meant that the carp were pretty clued up, and, although the water held good numbers of big fish, they wouldn't be a pushover if observation, baits and methods weren't up to scratch. On the other side of the coin, a number of good fish could be had each season if you were willing and able to put the necessary time and effort in and also willing to work at and get to grips with the techniques needed to put a few fish on the bank.

My initial approach for my first season on this water was to go in with boilies only and make use of much bigger than average baits. From what I could gather, this was not an approach that had been used on the venue in the past, and could be something different that would give me an edge if I could get on the fish on my visits to the water.

In fact, these tactics did work to an extent and I did have a couple of fish on the big fishmeal boilies during that first season. Still, I couldn't help but take note of the almost universal use of spodded hemp and corn by the water's more local and experienced carpers, and it was also difficult not to be impressed by the success that they had using this approach.

What was also hugely impressive was the accuracy and effectiveness of the majority of the carpers' use of the marker rod (or rods) and the precision and efficiency of the long-range spodding techniques. I was quick to discover that rubbing shoulders with more experienced and successful carp fishermen was a great way to learn, and this acted as a catalyst for improving my own methods and techniques.

As a direct consequence of these experiences I would recommend to anyone looking to improve their carp-catching capability that they fish a water where the experience and success of the majority of the members is higher than their own. It may be a bit daunting at first to know that your relative lack of ability may be exposed to others, but, as long as you go about discreetly observing and learning what other carpers are doing, your own skills and talents should quickly improve and increase in line with your confidence.

Catching on to Spodding

I decided to modify my approach to Pit 1 for the following season and start to look at the baiting methodology and spodding techniques used by some of the other syndicate members. I was keen to continue with a mainly boilie-based line of attack for my own fishing for several reasons, not least that I feel that regularly feeding the carp with a nutritious food item can only be good for their continued well-being. However, I couldn't ignore the success of the hemp and corn method, so I decided that this could perhaps be fished on one rod during the warmest months of the year, when it seemed to be at its most effective.

This also meant that I needed to improve my spodding tackle and technique. Previously I'd been able to bait up the spots I'd been fishing with a catapult or throwing stick, as I'd been using big 22–28mm boilies. Using smaller baits and

'Universe', at 43lb 10oz.

particles at range meant that a catapult and/or stick were impractical, and although I'd done a bit of spodding in the past it had always been with moderate amounts and at comfortable ranges. Although the distances involved would seem fairly modest to some of the more experienced guys, on Pit 1 I found that I needed to use a spod at ranges that I'd never managed before, and the kit I'd used in the past, made up from redundant pike and carping tackle and whatever spods I could lay my hands on, just weren't going to be up to the job.

Eventually I progressed to a purpose-built spod rod and became immersed in the quest for the perfect spod, but the major improvements were in my casting technique. Now, most experienced carpers witnessing my long-range casting technique would struggle to describe it as being either particularly elegant or efficient. Probably 'brutal' and 'just about adequate' would be closer to the truth. Eventually though, with timely advice and coaching from some of the lads and a bit of practice, and although my technique still wasn't pretty to watch, I could usually get a spod to reach most of the marks under most conditions.

Through a mixture of my own experiences and time spent at the pit and also talking to the other anglers, I gradually became aware of some rough patterns and trends in the captures and habits of some of the larger residents. It seemed to me that boilies tended to be slightly more selective for the bigger fish, and I learned that one fish in particular had never 'been out on the yellow stuff' (caught using corn/maize as a hookbait). This was a fish called Universe, a regular forty and the biggest fish in the pit at the time. It also appeared that some areas and swims on the pit produced more of the larger carp than other areas. There wasn't a swim on the pit that hadn't produced some of the larger carp at

some point in time, but there did seem to be certain areas that tended to throw up the big fish more regularly than others. As I was less interested in catching large numbers of fish than in getting to grips with the real biggies, and Universe in particular, I gradually evolved my tactics to suit. This involved restricting my swim selection to the swims that tended to throw up the biggies (unless I observed them elsewhere) and always ensuring that two out of the three rods allowed was adorned with a boilie hook bait. Not too long after adopting this methodology I landed Universe at a weight of 43lb 10oz on a boilie and from one of the swims I considered to be a good bet for the bigger fish.

On another occasion I was down on the pit for a three-night session, initially bivvied up in what I considered one of the big fish swims. Over the first couple of days things were relatively quiet, apart from a late evening and very early morning display of fish out from a nearby swim that I considered to be less of a big-fish-producing area. Observations actually appeared to back up my original thinking, as the fish showing in the swim didn't appear to be all that big (in relative terms) and didn't warrant me making a move despite the lack of action in my own swim. Eventually, however, the scenario appeared to change and the smaller fish showing on the spot looked to have been replaced by much bigger fish. Obviously I cannot be sure if this really was the case, but it did appear to me as if the smaller fish had been pushed out by a group of bigger fish that suddenly decided to take up residence. Now that the bigger fish were showing on the spot, a quick move to the vacant swim was called for. This appeared to pay off, as early the next morning I was jolted into consciousness as one of the rods roared off, and after a powerful scrap a mid-thirty was eventually resting in the folds of my landing net.

Some of the lads fishing the pit were also fastidious about the nature of the spot where a hookbait was going to be placed. They would map out the precise area very carefully with one or more marker float set-ups, and some lads would dismiss a spot if they subsequently detected even a tiny scrap of weed by casting the unbaited end tackle to the potential hookbait position. This appeared to be good practice and led to me being much more selective about placing my baits; I didn't go to the extremes some anglers appeared to favour, but I was much happier when there was no weed and/or other debris to affect bait presentation and the workings of the rig being used.

This is perhaps a suitable point to look at my marker and spodding set-ups in a little more detail…

The Marker and Spod Rods

For me the marker rod is almost as important as the rods that I'm using to present baits with.

With the exception of a bit of floater fishing and the odd bit of stalking, almost all of my stillwater carp fishing is undertaken with the prior use of a marker float to give me an idea of the depths and contours of the lake bed and weed growth.

It is probably fair to say that I don't do too much plumbing of the swim if I'm very familiar with it and I'm trying to keep disturbance to a minimum. However, this is rare, even on waters I've fished many times in the past.

Many people appear to object to the use of a marker float rod because of the potential scare factor, and to a certain extent I'd go along with that. Obviously churning the water to a foam by throwing a marker float attached to a heavy lead around the swim for an extended period of time can be a terrific way of scaring fish out of the swim. On the other hand, one of the best ways to

blank on any water is to chuck out a couple of baited end tackles indiscriminately, without a clue about the depths or features. Each situation has to be carefully weighed up before we automatically grab the marker rod out of the bag. If I already know that there are fish present in a swim and I'm fearful of spooking them, then I may settle for a couple of casts with the actual fishing rods and just a bare lead to ensure that the area I'm intending to cast a bait to is suitable. Or I may decide it's worth taking the risk of a few casts with a marker rod, using the smallest float and lead that I can get away with if I need to get some additional information regarding depth or need to place or mark a feature in the swim to aid accurate end tackle and bait introduction. We can perhaps conclude that in most circumstances, unless you can be certain of where to cast your baits, either by prior experience or from observing the fish, a few casts with the marker float are generally going to be of benefit.

So what am I trying to achieve by throwing the marker float around?

I've learned the hard way, by sitting behind rods with motionless indicators, that blindly whacking out the rigs to sit on weed and grime-covered spots is a large waste of time. In order to maximize the potential of any given swim it is good practice to discover the features and areas that will be attractive to the carp and that could hold plenty of natural food. Also, once our end tackles are in position, we need to be confident that our baits are clearly presented as we expect and that the rigs are not hung up or clogged with weed and detritus.

We can use the marker float set-up to show us a number of things, such as water depth, weed coverage and the approximate make-up of the lake bed. Putting these things together gives us a plan of the swim and should point the way to specific features and spots within the swim that are more likely to be attractive to a feeding carp than other, less appealing areas.

In a swim that I am unfamiliar with, I'd make a number of casts, fanning out each consecutive cast in an arch to ensure that the entire area that can be fished gets a rough mapping-out.

Towards the end of each cast, I hold the rod up and feather the line to help keep the line nice and straight between the lead/float and the rod tip. As the lead hits the water I trap the line, keeping it as tight as possible, and keeping the tip relatively high in the air. This helps me to feel the lead drop down through the water, and if the bottom is relatively firm, the rod tip will give a little nod and at the same time the lead will be felt to 'donk' as it hits the bottom. If the lead hits weed or lands in very soft silt, then you cannot feel it hit the bottom. This gives you an idea of the presence of weed and/or the composition of the bottom where you've just cast.

Tightening down to the lead and then letting out a foot of line at a time until the float reaches the surface gives you the depth of water at that spot.

Incidentally, many people advocate the use of a thick nylon monofilament link between the lead and run-ring to help allow the float to come up in the presence of heavy weed and/or 'chod'. I don't bother, as I'm relatively uninterested in spots where the weed/chod is that bad that it will inhibit the movement of the float. If the float refuses to rise, I either drag it back to an area that does allow it to move, or wind back in and cast to a different area.

On each cast, after the initial depth check, point the rod tip towards the marker and wind the float back down to the lead. When it's all tight, slowly sweep the rod tip back to the side and drag the lead along the bottom. You can feel the lead drag along,

The marker and spod rods: very important bits of kit in my mind.

and the different feel will give you an idea of what the lake bed is like.

If you're dragging through thick weed the float/lead will be difficult to move and will feel like it's snagging up – the heavy breaking strain braid is a bonus here. Thinner weed will not be as difficult to drag through, but will often feel as though it is snatching at the lead as progress is made in fits and starts. A clean sand or firm silt bed lets the lead smoothly glide over it, while the lead can be felt to tap and 'plink' over gravel as if it's tripping over a series of tiny little steps.

A braided mainline, although not entirely essential, is of immense help with transmitting these different sensations back down through the line and rod and back to the angler. This is mainly due to the lack of stretch when compared to monofilament lines, which tend to dull the associated feel and vibrations. When looking out for a braid to use as a line on the marker rod, it is wise to opt for something with a relatively high breaking strain, as the line will see plenty of use and will be dragged through innumerable weed beds and over gravel bars and suchlike over the course of a busy season. This is achievable without compromising the distance casting ability of the set-up as braided lines are inevitably thinner in cross-section than monofilament. Nowadays there are a number of braided lines specifically marketed for use with a marker rod set-up, and although they are expensive when compared to monofilament, they are so hard-wearing they can be utilized for a number of years before needing to be changed.

Generally, after each sweep of the rod, I'll make sure I'm pointing the rod at the float/lead and that everything is nice and tight before repeating the process of letting the float up a foot at a time to find the depth in the new spot.

The process of winding the float back to the lead, dragging the lead along with a slow sideways sweep of the rod and then charting the float's progress back to the surface should then be repeated as many times as it takes until the marker set-up has been retrieved back to your own margin. It is then time to make another cast to another area of the swim, or perhaps close to an area already charted to check out the extent of a particularly interesting feature.

Some of my friends use two marker rods when mapping out the features within a swim, as this undoubtedly gives a much clearer perspective regarding the extent of a feature. For example, a very clear idea of the length and even the direction of a small gravel bar can be obtained when you can place a marker float at both ends of a feature at the same time. The perspective is greatly reduced and a clear image much more difficult to obtain when only a single aspect of the bar can be observed at any one time. However, using an additional marker rod means there's going to be more kit to carry and set up and to my mind there is a practical limit to the amount of gear that I'm willing to cart around on any given session. Therefore, despite the obvious advantages of using more than one marker rod, I restrict myself to using just the one.

Most of the time, once a potential position for a hookbait has been identified, I pop a marker float up by the spot and then have a few exploratory casts around the general area with the rod that will potentially be used to present a bait in the area. These exploratory casts with the unbaited end tackle help to confirm the make-up of the lakebed and confirm the presence or otherwise of any weed etc that was previously identified using the marker rod set-up. Once the precise location of a spot for the hook bait has been decided upon, the mainline on the fishing rod can be marked, ensuring that casts can be made back out to the spot at the correct distance. If a spod is being used to get any free offerings out to the spot, then this can be marked up at the same time, helping to ensure that both the baited end tackle and the loose feed are recast out to the same area.

My first 'spod rod' was actually an old pike rod pressed into emergency service, rigged up with an old battered reel and thick mainline. It didn't take long for me to realize that a more suitable rod with a decent quality reel loaded with relatively thin mainline and a shock leader would be required if any distance and/or consistency were required.

In later years and after taking advice from more experienced spodders, my spodding kit eventually consisted of a purpose-built spod rod, a quality reel loaded with 8lb line (Diawa Sensor) and a tapered shock leader. This set-up has stood the test of time and is still my standard set-up today.

Fine-Tuning my Approach

Following the first couple of seasons carping at Elstow my tactics and methods became more defined, and consequently I only needed to make relatively minor alterations depending on the particular circumstances presented at the time. For a typical three-night session, my standard approach was to try to ascertain in which areas the larger fish may be taking up residence, usually with a combination of direct observation and talking to the lads already fishing. This was also weighed up against my preference for certain swims that had a history of producing the biggies.

The way the rota system worked between the two syndicate rotas meant that during the week, between around midday on Monday and midday on the Friday it could be fished by members from either rota. However, from Friday lunchtime up until the following Monday lunchtime it was exclusive to one rota or another on alternate 'weekends', with a draw for swims being made between the rota members that had turned up on the Friday morning.

Being on Rota B, I would usually time my arrival for early on the Sunday morning on a Rota B weekend. This gave me a good period to look for fish before deciding what swim to go for to fish the first night. Also, arriving on a Sunday meant that a good percentage of the anglers present would be packing up at some point during the day,

having fished over the weekend. This meant that as the pit gradually emptied, a fair number of good swims would be available to pick from. Furthermore, there was a 72-hour fishing rule, which meant that any anglers who had started on the Friday and were still fishing come the Monday would need to stop fishing and relinquish their swim by lunchtime, prior to the 'free for all' period open to members of both rotas, which started at noon. Using this to my advantage, if I felt that my initial choice of swims made on the Sunday wasn't the best, I was usually ready to defect to another swim at some stage on Monday morning.

Depending on the nature of the swim and any carp-related sightings, I'd try to pick either two or three separate spots to present the baits. I would bait up at least one of these spots using the spod rod with a good helping of hemp mixed with a sprinkling of corn and a double handful of both whole and chopped boilies. The spots baited with the spod mix would be fished with either one or two rods baited with either a maize or boilie-based hookbait fished on my little pop-up rig (see diagram). One of each type of hookbait was presented over the spod mix. The hookbait on the third rod would either be a boilie straight out of the bag fished as a standard bottom bait if the spot was weed-free, or a boilie rigged up on the little pop-up rig if there was a chance of a bit of weed being present. The third rod was rarely fished over the spod mix, just boilies – with the amount depending on the weather conditions and the amount of action observed on the spot.

The quality of the carp fishing that Elstow Pit 1 had to offer meant that I rarely fished for carp elsewhere. I'd very occasionally sneak the odd opportunist short session over on Pit 2. If the conditions looked favourable I'd have a quick

'Bruno' at 41lb+. The quality of the carp fishing was superb but it would soon be time to move on.

look over on Pit 2 and every now and then this would present an opportunity too good to miss. A bit of extra effort and a quick change of plans for an overnight session had the potential to turn up a very special bonus fish.

ESTATE LAKE

During the several years I fished at Elstow for the carp, I rarely carp fished elsewhere. However, I did receive an invitation to fish a large estate lake deep in the rolling Northamptonshire countryside on an infrequent basis, with usually either one or two overnight trips being offered each year. As these sessions were always to be in the company of a couple of good friends and were likely to provide some reasonable action if the conditions were good, they were difficult to turn down.

The stocks of fish were something of an unknown quantity but appeared to be reasonable in numbers. The biggest fish known to have been on the bank was an immaculate low thirty common, with the vast majority of the stock appearing to be made up of commons in the low double-figure bracket with a few bigger ones thrown in and a sprinkling of mirrors to add some variety.

The area of bankside that could be fished was severely limited, mainly due to the necessity of keeping the disturbance of the surrounding countryside to an absolute minimum, as the lake itself was situated in the middle of a very carefully managed game shooting estate. The fishable bankside was concentrated towards the deeper end of the lake, which fortunately contained some feature in the shape of a dam wall that could be fished from in places and a couple of small islands. One of the

A shot of the Estate Lake.

islands was close to the corner of the dam, the other way out at range and could only be reached with a hookbait cast from one particular area of bank, and then only if the wind was favourable. The majority of the lake bed was made up of silt that varied in depth and could either be virtually weed-free, or relatively weedy, depending on the time of year.

My friend Steve, who had gained me the invitation to fish the water, had enjoyed some success on previous trips using boilies following several prebaiting visits. As the fish were still fairly naïve I opted for a simple but adaptable approach for my first trip. This was based on baiting up a clear area at comfortable spodding/casting range that would be the target for a couple of hookbaits. A third rod was fished as a 'rover', either targeted at showing fish, or fished at maximum range out towards the distant island. The spod mix consisted of quite a large quantity of hemp and pellet with a good helping of corn and a few small 10mm fishmeal boilies mixed in.

Hookbaits fished over the spod were maize and half 10mm boilies fished on 'my little pop-up rig'. The hookbaits for the roving rod were heavily glugged pop-ups fished either as singles or with a stringer.

The target area for the spod was naturally chosen after careful use of the marker float and consisted of an area of medium depth, close to weed beds, but itself weed-free and with a firm rather than soft silt bottom at a range of around sixty-five yards. Not knowing quite how the fish would react to the spod, I took plenty of bait but held back on the initial introduction, knowing full well that further bait could be accurately introduced during the trip with the line on the spod rod clipped up at the required range.

Putting out the hookbaits and the initial spodding up was done by mid-afternoon, after which it was time to get the bivvy up and a kettle of water on the stove. No sooner had the first splash of boiling water hit the cup and I was away on the rod fishing maize in the middle of the spodded area. I was to learn that the carp in this particular water nearly all gave a very good account of themselves and this first fish was certainly no exception. Eventually it was in the net and I was soon weighing in a lovely-looking, mid-double-figure common.

As I'd scored so soon after the disturbance caused by the initial baiting, I took a gamble and introduced a further half dozen spods' worth of bait after casting back out. Carp came at intervals through the evening and, following a couple of hours' snatched sleep during the middle of the night, the indicators were back to life early the next morning. I soon developed something of a pattern where I'd top up the swim with a further half dozen or so casts with the spod rod after each fish. The first trip ended far too soon, and we were required to be packed up and away from the water by mid-morning. However, I'd had plenty of fish, ranging from low doubles to just over twenty pounds, had gone through nearly two buckets of spod, and, more to the point, had thoroughly enjoyed myself into the bargain.

One of a number of beautiful commons from the Estate Lake.

Part of a dream result on the Estate Lake.

Hectic Session

More trips to this wonderful venue followed in time, and one very hectic trip in particular stands out in my memory.

I'd carp-fished another water, a large gravel pit in the Nene Valley, the previous night. This was a club water virtually ignored by carpers, but with the potential to produce a very big fish. I'd fished a couple of overnight trips on previous occasions without any success, but on this occasion had caught a number of fish in a new swim. It hadn't produced the hoped-for biggie, but still the result was very pleasing and, though tired through lack of sleep, I was on a high as, back at home, I went about preparing yet more bait in readiness for the overnight trip to the estate lake.

Once I was at the estate lake it was difficult to curb my enthusiasm as I described to Steve the success from the previous night. Steve was pleased for me as always, but it was soon time to drag our tackle and buckets of bait to our prospective swims. On this occasion I'd taken even more bait than normal: it was mid-May, and with warm winds pushing towards my chosen swim, conditions looked good, and experience had shown that getting things right here in terms of both conditions and tactics was necessary to achieve a good number of fish on the bank. I actually had three buckets of spod with me, just in case, and had even more bait in the shape of dry pellet and boilies in the rucksack.

I was brimming with confidence because of the conditions and probably also

Elstow 1: not the most picturesque venue in the world.

because of the result on the club pit the previous night, so ended up putting out a fair amount of spod to my chosen spots in the first hit. However, as the afternoon wore on, it became apparent that I need not have worried about over-baiting, as the runs started to come from the baited spots at regular intervals. I'd abandoned the tactic of fishing one rod as a rover, as the results were far more consistent over the heavily baited areas. Therefore I tried to keep two separate areas of the swim topped up with spod and fished either one or two hookbaits on each spot as the amount of action on each spot dictated. I'd refresh the appropriate spot after each capture with several introductions of bait via the spod rod. This didn't seem to frighten the carp, even though the water wasn't particularly deep, at around six or seven feet. In fact, on more than one occasion I received a take while I was actually spodding, and I always ensured that I rebaited and put a fresh hookbait out to the spot before picking up the spod rod. The session became

quite demanding physically, as I was kept busy playing and landing fish, recasting end tackles and putting out more spod. On a couple of occasions I'd be playing one fish as another alarm would suddenly burst into action as a fish tore off on another rod.

The following morning I was dead on my feet. The action from the carp had barely relented all night and I had hardly managed any sleep at all. I wasn't about to complain, however, as a couple of singles, an absolute rake of doubles and a couple of scale-perfect 20lb+ commons to add icing to the cake was a dream result.

Following this particular session the action on the estate lake started to slow up. Although our visits remained very infrequent, it appeared that quite a number of others had managed to obtain permission to fish the water and pressure started to tell. Not only did the fish start to wise up, but they seemed to lose their previous immaculate condition, and the odd blemish and tatty fin started to appear. Not only this, but for some reason the weights appeared to be down on the average. I'm not sure why this might have been, as I'd have thought that anything the anglers introduced as way of bait would only supplement the natural food, but it did appear to be the case, and it transpired that a 20lb+ carp became a very rare fish indeed.

Preferring to remember the estate lake in its prime, with wonderful fish in stunning surroundings rather than witness a potential decline, I've not set foot on the bankside there for several years.

FINDING NEW WATERS

I eventually dropped my Elstow ticket for a number of reasons. One of those reasons was that there were new waters and different fish that I wanted to catch, and I didn't want my carp fishing to become stale and predictable.

Pit 1 at Elstow was an amazing place, not perhaps the most picturesque venue in the world, but the quality of the carp available must put the water towards the very top of the list of many carpers' most desirable venues to fish. Maybe someday I'd like to go back and renew my acquaintance with the place, but there are many new waters I'd like to fish and other desirable fish I'd like to catch.

It is important to make plans for the future if you want to fish syndicate waters or other venues that have membership restrictions of one sort or another. Making a phone call or writing a letter to place yourself on a waiting list requires comparatively little time and effort, but I'm amazed at how few people are willing to put even this amount of effort into obtaining a ticket that they desire. Often these same people are only too willing to moan about the quality of the fishing that is available to them and are quick to point out how

'lucky' others are to have such good venues at their disposal. Because in the past I've planned for the future, for a number of years now I've been in the fortunate position of having a number of good waters that I can fish. In the past I've made the effort to be known to fishery owners and ensured that I've been placed on waiting lists for waters I wanted to fish. Obviously this is something that needs to be an ongoing activity as the waters you want to fish change over the years.

A bit of common sense also helps to secure those most coveted tickets. It's

I am not afraid of putting a bit of bait in when I feel that it is advantageous.

113

worth being on your best behaviour when at the waterside, and even if I'm tired and suffering from a series of blanks, I try to make an effort to display a positive and helpful attitude in front of others.

Getting yourself a reputation as a bit of a troublemaker or for being dishonest or uncaring is never going to make yourself popular with your fellow anglers and will never go down well with fishery owners or managers. Being known for having a bad attitude isn't the sort of reputation you want following you around when you're looking to gain admission to new waters and are out to make a good impression on those responsible for vetting the membership. It makes good sense to display sensible behaviour towards both the environment and fellow carpers when on the bank and a

friendly, caring attitude can only add to the pleasant experience we are all looking for when we're out fishing.

It's always worth keeping yourself plugged into the carp fishing 'grapevine' so long as the sharing of information is a reciprocal arrangement and you're not divulging information that's not really yours to share. I always try to keep myself well informed with details of significant captures and up and coming waters.

Two Gravel Pits, Two Approaches

As part of this information gathering, details of a particular southern gravel pit and the carp it contained started to stir my imagination. Over a similar period a couple

Waiting for action on the local pit. Note the spod and marker rods to the side of the swim.

A huge common: my mate Richard with the fish at 57lb+ that was caught in early autumn 2005.

of the bigger, stunning-looking commons stocked into a gravel pit closer to home had also grabbed my attention as they packed on the weight over the following years.

A ticket for the southern pit was going to prove difficult to get hold of. As it happened, a bit of prior planning and a measure of good fortune eventually resulted in the offer of a ticket.

The new gravel pits, as all new waters do, had their own unique set of problems to overcome and moods and vagaries to learn and cater for. Both pits could become busy, not surprisingly, considering the quality of carp they contained, and, as on other venues, being creative and making the effort to either arrive early or be looking and listening for fish activity when most would be tucked up either in bed or in the bag, tended to pay dividends.

Making the extra effort to arrive very early in the morning nearly always paid off

in the warmer months of the year. This was especially true on the southern pit. It meant having hardly any sleep that night if I was to travel to the water, get parked up and be sitting perched on a bucket at a prime observation spot before first light. However, this was a great time to spot those subtle signs of fish activity during those periods when the carp weren't keen to make a big display of their whereabouts. The odd head and shoulder or something similar during the first hour of daylight would sometimes be the only telltale sign of where the majority of the big fish were resident. If I was quick I could have a couple of rods out from a vacant swim and be in with a shout of a morning take before most of the carpers were out of their sleeping bags.

Locating fish at night was another useful tactic, especially on the more local pit. Obviously direct sightings were difficult, but the carp could at times become quite active and make plenty of noise jumping and rolling. The trick here was to try to make out the size of the fish from the noise they made. A night with perfect conditions could result in carp activity being heard from several different areas. The really big fish do tend to make quite a distinctive sound at times, and moving into a swim where it sounded as if hippos had been rolling around during the night was always a good bet for the bigger fish.

On the local pit I was very much interested in one fish in particular, a huge common that by most accounts had been stocked weighing in the low twenties and had continued to grow 'like stink' over the years that followed. This particular fish is in my eyes a real looker and is of a size that really makes you sit up and take notice. Therefore, despite there being a number of other very desirable fish to have a go for, I felt that all my efforts on this particular venue needed to be geared towards putting this one particular fish on the bank.

The southern pits called for a different approach. Although I obviously wanted to catch the bigger carp, most of which were mirrors, it didn't appear as if there were many ways to separate the habits and preferences of the bigger fish from the smaller ones. Despite one of the biggies appearing to show a preference for picking up baits in one particular area of one particular swim during the early and later part of the season, I couldn't find any other pattern to location that would help to be selective towards the larger carp.

In order to put the big common on the bank, I looked at both patterns in location and bait preferences to help shorten the odds and make my time on the venue the most productive I could. I selected the times of year when I could be at the pit the most, also taking into account the possibility of doing overnighters between work,

and selected the swims preferred by the common at these times of year to concentrate on. Looking back on previous captures showed that the big common liked its boilies, particularly fishmeal-based baits. It appeared to be most likely to be caught on a boilie fished over a bed of similar free offerings, either with or without fishmeal-based pellets. It didn't appear at all keen on seed-based particles and wasn't terribly likely to pick up a boilie fished over the top of a bed of particles. After a brief experiment with a particle bed for one rod on overnighters that produced only 'average'-sized fish, the particles were ditched for this particular venue and baiting strategy was based on either boilies or a boilie/pellet combination. Naturally this wouldn't prevent other fish picking up a hookbait intended for the biggie, but it did appear to cut down on the amount of action, helping to keep things settled and ready for the big one to make an appearance. An added bonus was that fish caught using this approach tended to be of a high average size, mostly weighing in at the upper twenties or more.

Of course the boilie and pellet approach is both popular and well practised by today's carpers, with an endless number of baiting options that can be brought into play. One of these options involves putting out a big bed of bait with a number of hookbait presentations, often using pop-ups to present hookbaits over the bed of bait. I fancied using this approach whenever practical, but only when the chance of a session in a favoured swim was possible. I don't feel confident in this tactic when I'm unsure of the swim or if time is limited. It's certainly not something I'd recommend for an overnighter or a session where I'm likely to be changing swims.

A typical example of using this tactic was one session where I had three nights in front of me and was able to get myself into

A scale-perfect linear.

a swim that I fancied for the big common. Once I'd reminded myself of the features and had charted the latest weed growth with the marker float set-up, I was ready to start introducing the bait. I'd decided to use Dynamite's Halibut Pellet boilies as the basis for this big bed of bait session, as I could mix both shelf life and frozen boilies in a mixture of sizes, together with halibut pellets in a mixture of sizes, which would give me a bed of baits of different sizes and rates of decomposition.

First of all I had to get the bait out into the swim. I'd decided to really go for it, as the conditions looked good for a feeding spell and using really big beds of bait isn't a tactic that is used very often, even on popular waters. Finally, after around three hours of almost non-stop spodding, I had got 12kg of bait, split fifty-fifty between boilies and pellet, spodded out and had drawn more than the odd curious look from fellow anglers in the process!

The first night was a blank, but night number two produced a very pretty and

heavily scaled mid-thirty, one of the most sought-after fish in the lake. It wasn't the big common, but I was well pleased with that fish and obviously pleased to see the baiting tactic produce the goods. The next session was only a two-nighter, but I was confident in the swim and the conditions again looked good, so a good helping of bait – 8kg of Dynamite Halibut pellet and boilies – was again spodded out to my chosen spot. Again, the big common failed to make a mistake, but another big fish weighing well over thirty pounds found itself in the bottom of the landing net before it was time to pack up.

Tactics on the southern pit were very different. The pit was a relatively busy one, fished by a number of very experienced anglers, and the fish were subsequently well clued up. After some experimentation, I found the method best suited to the amount of time I could spend on the water was to use two different approaches between the two rods allowed. Tiger nuts were one of the going baits at the time, and

117

Night number two produced a very pretty and heavily scaled mid-thirty.

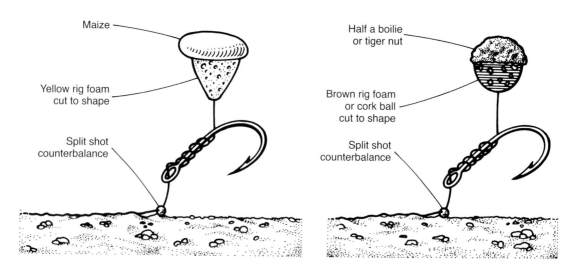

My little pop-up rig.

I'd like the left-hand indicator to roar off now!

I used a tightly spodded bed of mixed particles containing a small handful of chopped tigers on one rod, using my little pop-up rig with half a tiger nut fished over the top.

On the other rod I usually fished a single 12mm fishmeal boilie, either cut in half and again presented on my little pop-up rig or fished as a straight bottom bait, depending on what the lake bed was like and if there was any weed. If at all possible, I fished the boilie rig closer in and introduced free bait via a catapult. If the spot was further out then I would use a spod to introduce the freebies, usually about a double handful of boilies at a time.

Huge beds of bait were going to be counterproductive for me on this particular venue. The carp tended to be on the spooky side and quite mobile. Therefore a 'softly, softly' approach, small beds of bait and a willingness to move swims were called for.

Owing to a number of other commitments, I ended up fishing only a handful of sessions on this particular water. However, using the tactics and strategies outlined I have enjoyed a measure of success more often than not and put a number of good fish on the bank, including mirrors of over thirty pounds and a common of over thirty-seven pounds.

CONCLUSION

I've enjoyed looking back at some of the waters I've carp-fished in the past, and recalling some of the challenges that have been presented along the way. There may be parallels with your own fishing and possibly even lessons to be learned from the details of some of the changes I've made to my own approach to suit various circumstances, and from the recounting of some of my past experiences. Whatever the case, I hope you've enjoyed reading what I've written.

Tight lines.

4. Mastering Difficult Carp Waters

by Graham Kent

A DAY IN THE LIFE OF A CARP ANGLER

Beep, beep, beep! My alarm clock wakes me well before light. An hour later I finally drag myself up, make a flask, grab my bait and I'm on the road. Driving early morning is almost a pleasure but my mind is totally on the day ahead. I haven't had a carp for over a month but saw one bosh last trip in a bland, deeper area. It's a start and the first sighting in a while. What way is the wind blowing? How warm is it? I know you shouldn't have preconceived ideas on swim choice but I normally do: shall I fish the lawn or maybe Prat in the hat?

On arrival the fifteen-acre pit looks great, not a breath of wind and the chance maybe to find some bubblers. I dump the gear on the lawn and have a walk round, only a quick one as I want my baits in ASAP. Wish I'd got up when the alarm went, A few bream roll near a plateau at sixty yards but the twenty-five or so carp that the lake holds are nowhere to be seen, as usual, so one rod lands near the bream – after all, they're feeding on something – and the other rod on the spot of the bosher from the week before. Rigs are mono hook length with an inch and a quarter fine hair, and the bait a home-made fish-meal full of goodies. I have great faith in both, so I forget about them and focus only on where to put them.

Three hours and three bream later, the sun is up and I think about moving. The pit is looking blue now with the reflection of the sky, and a light breeze has sprung up. I wind the rods in and give the pit a proper circuit; it's looking like tap water, and from various trees I can see shoals of roach going about their business and the odd pike resting in the sanctuary of the branches. I don't check every tree, as time has taught me that the carp only frequent specific ones. Good job really, as otherwise it could take me all day.

Approaching the shallows, I see my first carp. It's a low twenty common and is moving very fast towards the deeper far end. They've been like this all year, very agitated on the shallows. In years gone by, it's been a good area but not any more – I think they've sussed it. After a good look round and no more sightings it's time for a think. Prat in the Hat is a good option as you can see most of the lake, but I did see a carp on the shallows. I decide to fish the edge of the shallow area where it drops off to about eleven feet. This swim gives me the chance to see if any other fish move through the channel into the other half of the pit. I travel light so I'm installed in the area in minutes. One chuck with the marker to confirm what I already know and out with the baits followed by twenty freebies on each, then time to relax with a coffee and a smoke.

The Prat in the Hat swim was good to me.

Unfortunately, the day is getting brighter than I'd hoped, but today is the only day I've got free this week and beggars can't be choosers. During the next hour I receive two small line bites. Maybe I'm on fish, time will tell. Wham – the left-hand rod is flying. Just a tench. Oh well, at least it got me all excited for a while. A couple of hours drift by with no more occurrences so I become restless. These carp are catchable but getting on them is the hard part. Time for another move, so I wind in and spend the next hour looking. Nothing. It could be worse, at least I'm not at work. With nothing to go on, I decide on the secret swim area. This spot is in the northeast corner with a couple of promising overhanging trees, often worth a go in the afternoon sun. Although nothing is showing they might be just a tad further out.

One bait is dropped in six foot at the end of the trees with a sprinkling of pellet, while the other rod is whacked out towards an island on a high viz. You just never know. It's getting very warm and I doze off; I must be getting old. When I come to, the bobbins are as I left them – no liners, nothing. A coffee gets my head together and I must decide where to spend the last few hours before dark and home time. I end up back where I started, on the lawn. As the light fades into evening the bream and the odd tench start to show again. These fish are rolling in the exact same spot as they were in the morning. Something has got to be going on in the area, maybe a hatch.

One of the regulars turns up and I'm no longer alone on the pit. He's down for his thirty-first night and so far he's had no carp to show for his efforts. We have a chat mainly questioning our sanity, especially when four miles down the road is a puddle with seven thirties in it, but we agree that a double from here is easily as good if not better than the pay and display carp. With our blanking justified, he barrows his gear to the shallows and no doubt asks himself whether bloodworm pellets are the answer, or if he should try the new super-duper rig he's just read about.

It's a lovely evening and I'm cursing the fact that I've got to go home, but I have work tomorrow so there's no choice. Wonder what state the house is in? The boys have been home alone all day and I haven't a clue what to give them for dinner. Bleep, drop back on right-hand rod and another six-pound bream is winched in. Don't mind too much, at least I know the bait's edible. I make tracks and tell the carp that they are in big trouble next Sunday, just wait. Silly hobby.

THE JOY OF DIFFICULT WATERS

So why fish difficult waters when there are so many lakes heaving with big carp? For me personally the lake I catch carp from is far more important than the sheer size or number of carp I can accumulate in a season. To me, a rarely caught double that's grown up in some wild, windswept pit is worth far more than Gerty the thirty that gets caught every Friday night. The harder the lake, the greater the satisfaction when the bobbin finally whacks the butt. The longer the wait, the more rewarding the capture. It's not for me, sitting on busy lakes being bombed by spods and marker floats. I find the fewer carp a water holds, the fewer carp anglers are on it. You escape the numbers game and catch carp with both lips still intact. It's each to their own, I know, but whenever I fish a lake and catch too many I become bored and move on. Carp fishing in the old days was a challenge, and that's how I still like it.

When I'm on runs water and not catching I become frustrated and fidgety, generally getting more fed up as each hour passes. On difficult lakes you are not supposed to get takes so I find I can relax and blame the stock levels for my lack of action as opposed to my rubbish angling ability.

One thing that fascinates me is the uncaught carp that the lakes hold where I fish. It seems to be the same old fish that come out, but occasionally I've stumbled across a group of big carp that to my knowledge have never been caught. Why these fish never end up on the bank, I really don't know. Are they smarter than the friendly ones, feed in a different way, in different areas, or after a lifetime of growing big by eating creepy-crawlies do they simply not recognize our offerings as food? The dilemma is: do you persevere in the faint hope that one might make a mistake and put up with repeat captures of the friendly ones, or do you move on? I've come to the conclusion that I will never fully understand carp.

My friend James Parry has fished Castle Waters for years and hasn't caught any of the huge fish it contains. He's seen them on many occasions but hasn't even hooked one. I'm not talking a few trips here and there, but a ten-year obsession. Is it down to bait? The smaller fish up to just touching thirty seem happy to pick up the odd tiger nut while the monsters are just not getting caught. Although these carp have reached a very large size without bait, you wouldn't think that they would turn down an easy meal. The truth is, if we did know all the answers, carp fishing would be very boring indeed.

IN THE BEGINNING

Of all the waters local to me at the time, the Spoon reservoir was the only lake with a known big fish. It had a reputation for being seriously rock hard, but with a biggie at stake it had to be done. The reservoir was called the Spoon because of its shape, its real name was Ecclesbourne Reservoir and it was run by the local Clive Vale angling club. The bowl of the Spoon was concrete lined with the slabs going out for around three or four rod lengths, where it then became a normal lake with silt and gravel. The handle of the Spoon slowly narrowed up till it terminated at a reed-infested feeder stream. All in all, the water covered about three acres.

So what makes a small water like this so difficult? It certainly wasn't angling pressure, as most of the time I was the only one carp fishing. It was simply the stock levels. As far as I could ascertain, three mirrors were stocked by the club in the 1950s;

these came from another water, called Pett Pools, and at the time of stocking they weighed between two and four pounds. The rest of the stock consisted of a handful of commons between five and fourteen pounds. The low stock of carp wasn't the only problem, as the Spoon also contained a fair few tench and, worst of all, shedloads of good-sized bait-pinching bream.

The campaign began. The first plan of action was to get some bait in. I baited twice a week with a few hundred baits each time. At first it was spread around but gradually I narrowed it down to two spots I fancied. These were a corner filled with pads and the reedy end of the handle. The bait was based on a 50 per cent Casilan mix and flavoured with cinnamon leaf oil. It was a bait I had caught loads of fish on in other waters and, as it was given to me by the great man himself, Fred Wilton, I knew I could forget about the bait and concentrate on finding the fish.

Night-times were hopeless – bream after bream after tench after bream – so in the end I gave up and just fished days; far more civilized. The end of the handle was looking to be the best bet, since, being fairly shallow, the bream tended to avoid it in daylight; and at least the carp had a chance of finding the bait if it was still lying on the bottom rather than in the mouth of a bream. Both sides of the swim were lined with overhanging trees and I often cast my baits to the point where the reeds hit the treeline. Tackle consisted of 11ft, 1½lb test curve Jack Hilton rods, 11lb Sylcast and No. 2 Jack Hilton carp hooks. Rigs, although pretty irrelevant today, consisted of a simple link ledger, a half-ounce lead and a side-hooked bait. You might well laugh, but at the time most people were using paste baits with the hook buried inside. Side-hooking was cutting edge, as were boilies. I remember Rockabilly Roy walking into my swim just as I was about to cast

At last. I could now move on to a lake that contains more than two mirrors.

out and saying, 'Hold on, Gray, your bait's falling off.' 'That will be all right,' I said as I lobbed it along the tree line. Roy was none the wiser, bless him.

After half a dozen day trips it happened. The bottle top whacked up and I was in. Talk about a tug of war. My old Hiltons were bent straight as I hung on for dear life. The reel was moving around on the corks beneath and then, just as I thought all was lost, it was – the fish had snagged me in the trees. Only one thing for it, strip down to my pants and in I went. It was a lot deeper than I imagined but by holding onto the branches I managed to pull myself along until finally my feet touched the lake bed. After following the line I came to my

ledger stop. I tell you, it's a bit scary sliding your hand down the line knowing that the biggest carp of your life is only inches away. Well I say inches, it was more like three hundred yards, as the hook was firmly embedded in a branch.

A few million sessions later the same happened again. Bottle top did its thing but this time I won. In my net lay the second biggest carp in the lake, a lovely old grey mirror. I was well chuffed, but it was not the object of my desire. Oh well, back to spending all my money on Casilan. I knew that one day we would meet face to face so I kept going.

By now the reeds had encroached on my spot and I thought I might have to stalk it under the trees. With this in mind I carried a boat rod with 25lb line in my bag just in case. In late August an opportunity arose. In a little gravel clearing behind the reeds and trees, the monster lay. I went back to my swim for the boat rod but instead I just wound about fifteen yards of the heavy line onto my Mitchell 410 and tied on a No. 2, which was no mean feat in itself as the line was about the same diameter as the eye of the hook. When I crept back, to my dismay the carp had gone and a small common had taken her place. Plop, a small stone landed on the common's head, dealing with that problem. With no sign of the big girl, I just dropped the boilie on the gravel clearing and prayed. I remember the line being so curly it spiralled through the rings and all the way to the bait. The carp gods were on my side, as she appeared over the bait. I could make out the orange belly and a few scales along her back but couldn't see if she'd picked up the bait or not. Slowly the carp backed off, but more importantly my line followed. Whack, and all hell broke loose. I didn't have room to play the fish so I just jumped in after it. I found myself sitting on the gravel clearing up to my waist in water holding my line and a bemused carp swimming between my legs. I just grabbed it and staggered up the bank.

Petra, as the fish was later named, was a beauty. The scales showed her to be a personal best and a lake record. At last I could fish other lakes again that actually had some carp in them. I found it interesting that I didn't hook any of the commons on the milk protein bait but a couple of years later had a few on particles. I found the same thing happened a few years later at Yateley when the HNV caught the mirrors but none of the smaller commons that outnumbered the mirror carp.

Petra is still alive to this day.

Footnote: I would no longer consider trying to catch a carp from such a snaggy area. Luckily for me Petra wasn't hurt. I no longer agree with hook and hold jungle stick type tactics.

BIG PIT VIRGINS

Why Pete, Roy and I decided to fish Nichols quarry at Hythe when we did, I do not know. After years on small intimate lakes of no more than three or four acres and thinking we'd got it sussed, the eighty-acre pit brought us back down to earth with a bang. First thing we did was to spend the day in a rubber dinghy plumbing, and we were glad we did. In places it went down to eighteen feet and in others the lake bed came up to within two feet of the surface. It took us all day and was hard work but we gained an awful lot of knowledge. It was very different from the relatively flat-bottomed, silty estate lakes. Before we started my gear had to be sorted. I couldn't get away with fifty yards of line on my reels any more, and big leads were the order of the day. Bait wise, we used our tried and tested Wilton bait, milk proteins and an essential oil label. We didn't bother pre-baiting, as none of us had any money and a few kilos here and there would have had very little effect, especially as the pit was full of bream. Big baiting campaigns are no doubt beneficial and great if you're sponsored, but for average anglers like us it was a non-starter.

On 15 June we were all set up waiting for midnight. Things were looking rosy, with carp showing in front of my northeast corner. I'd never seen fish bosh like it, a constant stream of carp leaving the water and having fun. I couldn't wait to cast out but as the evening began to draw in and we got closer to the witching hour, the wind died down and started to blow the other way. The carp went with it and I should have

Pete Radley with his first Hythe carp.

followed. It doesn't take a genius to recognize the importance of wind on large waters. Lesson 1: follow the wind. The first problem we faced was trying to get the freebies out. The catapults were totally inadequate, and with the fish showing out of range the only option was to whack out a single hook bait. I couldn't believe it when I had a take on a single 15mm bait

cast ninety yards to a showing fish when the nicely baited sixty-yard spot produced nothing. This pit was to teach us a lot very quickly. If you are not on them you won't catch them, and it doesn't matter if you've a baited patch – if the carp don't want to go there they won't. That day, one bait in the right place was more productive than two hundred in the wrong one.

126

The first take was a 19lb 4oz mirror. Then, twenty-four hours later, without another bite apart from bream, it was obvious even to a big pit virgin like me that a move was on the cards. Pete and I headed straight to the windward bank. At the time Nichols had a huge spit that formed two bays at the southern end. Pete, being Pete, got the end of the spit and I fished up the side. The strange thing is that normally if you have a spit or point on a pit, the bar should in theory run off in the same direction but our close season plumbing had told us differently and it in fact ran off to the left. Pete set up and cast about sixty yards, landing in twelve feet of water. I had a shallow area in front of me coming up to about six feet with seventeen feet all around this shallow bar. More by luck than judgement we were on fish, and the takes were soon forthcoming. It soon became obvious that our casts had to be spot on, and if we landed in the deeper water our baits remained uneaten.

It was during this session that I discovered the countdown technique, something I have done with every single cast made since. By casting out and stopping the lead just before it hits the water the lead can be counted down until you feel it hit the bottom. This enables you to plumb the depth with every cast. It doesn't really matter how fast you count so long as it's the same speed every time. If you have a take from a cast that took, say, five seconds to reach the bottom and your next cast also lands on a five-second spot, you know you are in the taking depth. Most of our fish were coming

In 1981 Hythe was very different from today. There were only a handful of big 'uns but they were crackers.

in depths between four and six seconds, any more or less produced very little. This technique can also tell you if you are landing on hard or soft bottom or even weed, and stopping the lead at the right time causes the hook length to fly past the lead and helps to avoid tangles. It's brilliant. If you become really proficient at this you can almost lay your lead on the surface, causing far less disturbance.

Rigs consisted of a 10in mono hook-length with a 1½in, 2lb nylon hair tied to the eye. This was the first time I'd ever used the hair-rig. Thanks to big Steve for showing me the rig – it gave me a serious edge over all the other anglers. Imagine being the only angler on a lake using boilies and the hair today. That's what I call an edge. It makes me laugh when people talk about edges nowadays. If you think using

Castle Waters – a hundred acres and only Roy and I carp fishing it. Bliss.

different size pellets in your PVA bag is an edge you don't know what an edge is. Due to the massive undertow and winds we started to clip up by making line clips from matchsticks and insulation tape. Roy had a bit of trouble with this method. He would often wind in in the morning only to find a bream on the end that hadn't managed to pull the line out of the clip. Basically he had been livebaiting a 4lb bream all night, and live bream are not the best of carp baits.

There were times when the fish seemed to go missing and could only be located by fishing various different areas. I found a concentration of carp towards the end of October and had a good hit, including the scaly one for the first time, and they never really moved from that area all winter, which was handy. I've since fished other large pits and the same has often applied, as long as the angling pressure is low.

I remember a day in November when Pete got the hump. He had a tangle or something and in a blind rage threw his expensive carbon rod on the grass and kicked it as hard as he could. Luckily for him he was useless at football and he missed saving his rod from an early grave. His rod was safe but his boom 80 moon boot flew off his foot and landed thirty yards out in to the pit: a classic angling moment. My advice for fishing big pits in winter is not to kick your rods unless you have a spare pair of boots with you.

One thing that amazed me about this eighty-acre hole in the ground was the number of repeat captures. Pete had a 21lb common twice, I had the scaly one 3 times and I'm sure Roy doubled up with some of his bream; mind you, it's a job to tell as they all look the same. The repeat captures told us that the pit in fact only held a small number of decent-sized carp. This brought home to us the importance of actually being on carp, which still applies today in any low-stock venue.

During the quiet spells we started to doubt our baits. The bait was changed to an Equivite milk pellet boilie. The bait produced a few carp but the main problem was eels, who loved the stuff. Rockabilly Roy had them to 4lb 8oz; mind you, it probably made a change from bream. A 40 per cent Robin Red bait caught a few but in the end I went back to milk protein, substituting the essential oil for a synthetic butter flavouring. Thinking bait was the problem was a mistake – the reason for lack of action was down to location. By the end of the season we had all learned an awful lot, which is the advantage of fishing different types of waters.

The Importance of Bait

OK, I hold my hands up, I'm a bait freak and have nearly always made my own. I say my own, but I've been lucky to spend time and share findings with some very good bait men. In 1977, Malcolm Streeter showed me Robin Red. In 1978 I spent time at Johnson's with Fred Wilton and was shown the way with milk proteins and essential oils. In the 1980s Steve took me further down the path of knowledge, and nowadays I work on bait with Kevin Woodrow of Yateley fame. All these great anglers have unselfishly shared their know-how with me and I will be eternally grateful to them.

The disadvantage of making your own bait is the hassle of rolling thousands of boilies, but the advantages are tenfold. Your own bait is usually unique, it can be tweaked for size, buoyancy, flavour levels, texture, colour – the list is endless. Probably best of all is the satisfaction gained when the bobbin flies up on a bait you've put together yourself. It's a lot harder today to have an edge as far as bait is

Kev Woodrow with a previously uncaught thirty.

concerned because many of the shop-bought baits are very good, but in the back of my mind I've always had a little niggle when using them. If I catch a good fish on, say, a Nash bait, who actually caught the carp – me or Gary Bayes? Don't get me wrong, I am not knocking all the carp captures on commercial baits, but for me,

personally, for them to count it's got to be on my own bait. Catching on a home-made bait is comparable to catching a trout on a home-tied fly. It simply adds to the pleasure. One thing I do know is that my most successful baits have caught a lot of nuisance fish such as tench and bream. A good bait catches all species.

130

Kev, top bait man.

I could write down a few recipes that have brought me success over the years, but there's not a lot of point really, as you would be catching on my bait and so defeating the object, so here are a few general observations. One thing for sure is that a good bait is always a good bait, and much of what has gone before is still very relevant today. Robin Red was and still is superb. I used it as 40 per cent of the mix in the late 1970s and still do. It goes well with all manner of flavours from spicy oils to Premiers plum. On pressured waters I like the red unflavoured, just relying on the base mix.

Fishmeals are very good on all waters. Green-lipped mussel is fantastic and I use it at 5 per cent of my mix. It would be even higher if I could afford it. I like to use at least 60 per cent fishmeal in a mix, the rest being milks and binders. Pre-digested fishmeal is good stuff to have in a mix. We won't go into the science but its smell and taste complements any fish mix. Fishytype attractors, such as Monster Crab and Shellfish Sense Appeal, have always worked well for me in a fishmeal base. Today I tend to rely on natural attractors such as shrimp derivatives, various fish sauces or liquidized creatures such as lugworm or cockles.

Milk proteins were and still are very good carp catchers. One big plus is that they are out of vogue, so by using them you can offer the carp something different – always a plus point. The problem with milks is that good-quality ingredients are hard to source and you really don't know if your casein is any good until you use it. This is the main reason that many of the earlier milk baits were based on 50 per cent Casilan, which is expensive but reliable. As with fish or birdfood baits, I like the attractors to complement the base mix and have done well using the out-of-fashion creamy or butter-type tastes.

The scope for experiment is endless and many hours can be enjoyed when you can't get out fishing just surfing the net for ingredients or talking bait on the phone with your like-minded chums. Even that boring trip to the supermarket can take on a whole new dimension when you've got bait ingredients on your mind.

Are home-made baits any better than shop-bought ones? Well, the answer is that sometimes you hit on a really good bait and have it away big style, but there are also times when an established commercial bait will out-fish you. When a lot of anglers are all baiting with the same proprietary boilie you will probably only catch your share and no more. All bait makers strive for the ultimate bait, but in reality it would be a very sad day for carp angling if this goal was ever achieved. So I roll bait purely for personal satisfaction. They are generally fairly complex, but don't overlook the simple ones such as trout pellet boilies. Pete, Roy and I have had some right results over the years on trout pellets. The locals thought we were on amino acid attractors. Why did they think that? Well because that's what we led them to believe.

So we have our bait and now we have to apply it. I don't usually pre-bait simply because I can't be bothered to make up loads of bait. If I do put a bit in, it's normally only small amounts in places that I know the carp like to frequent. All the above comments apply to boilie fishing, mainly because I enjoy this style of fishing more than most, but I've done my fair share with particles. I used them in quantity on low-angling-pressure venues generally when I have time on my hands. This is a rarity, so most of my fishing is short-session day trips and I've always had better results using baits sparingly. Normally one or two pouchfuls are more than enough. I recently spent the day on a busy, well-stocked day ticket water and couldn't believe the amount of spods bombarding the lake. I felt as though I was taking part in a bizarre spodding competition. There was a knock-on effect; every time an angler began spodding the rest followed. The lake bed of this particular pit must be constantly covered with seeds and pellets. There is no doubt that the carp are cleaning it all up but takes are fairly few and far between. Carp can drop down almost anywhere for a mouthful of food and I'm sure takes only occur when a carp happens to drop down right over a hook bait. I don't know how many thousands of items are in a spod, but multiply that by ten or twenty spodfuls and multiply that again by the number of spodders on the lake, and you have an awful lot of food items. We must be

A quality old Leney on a quality bait.

making it hard for ourselves. Imagine the whole lake covered in chum mixer, what chance has your hookbait? Luckily I mostly spend my time on lakes containing very few carp and even fewer carp anglers and manage to avoid this scenario.

Get the amount of freebies or spods right and the fish will soon end up on your hook. Get it wrong and you wait for ages. So how much is right? Sometimes you just get a feeling about it. There are days when they want loads of bait but there are also times when a stringer will do. To start with, I like to have a different baiting pattern on each rod until I find the successful one. If I'm using three rods the going method will

be used on two rods but I'd probably still play around with the third. A hookbait and three free offerings gave me a great few months on an estate lake near Tonbridge. I usually play it on the safe side. It is possible to get away with too little bait but not so good if you've overdone it.

A TALE OF TWO THIRTIES

So where are we going this year, Pete? How about Yateley? It's got a forty in it and the pictures I've seen of the place, well, it's handsome. So Yateley it was. I thought Yateley was one lake, and couldn't believe it when the £16 tickets turned up and I discovered that there was actually thirteen or more lakes on the complex. After doing my homework I decided on the match lake. It held a good head of upper doubles and twenties, enough, hopefully, that I might catch one. The lake was even big enough to accommodate Pete's casting. He's famous for chucking them all over the place.

Our first trip was soon upon us and after a quick look round, I changed my mind completely and decided on the Copse. The Copse Lake was like the ultimate pit but in miniature. Secluded bays, gravel bars, weed beds, islands – it had the lot yet was still only around three acres. It had a very intimate nature and the stock consisted of about ten mirrors and quite a few small commons. The main beauty of Yateley Copse Lake was that the carp behaved like carp should. From the top of the many climbing trees you could watch them drifting up to the shallows for the afternoon and then back towards the deeper end to spend the night: classic.

Bait was a Casilan, granular Pruteen (the powder version was hopeless) and a wheatgerm mix, flavoured with 5ml to four eggs of Geoff Kemp's juicy plum, rounded off with 2ml of dense sweetener. It was the real McCoy. I normally ended up fishing four or five swims during the course of a day trying to set my little traps just before the carp arrived. This moving around worked a treat, resulting in little pockets of my bait dotted all around the lake. The carp soon found it, and it wasn't long before my bottle tops were flying.

There were two real biggies in the Copse. One was the Parrot, and the other, a fish that few people believed existed, called the Pineapple. I saw them together on several occasions and estimated them both to be around mid-thirties.

I was on my way to the copse for a couple of days' fishing, but while walking past the match lake, it just looked right so I gave it a go. I chucked out two rods in peg twelve, seventy baits round each and set my net up. Turning around, I saw my reel spinning. Result – a mid-twenty after about five minutes on the complex. I knew it was a fluke so I carried on to the Copse.

At the time the fish were starting to show in the middle from around 7.30am till maybe 10am. So out went seventy baits followed by my hookbaits and I settled in for what I knew would be a quiet night. I just wanted it all ready for the morning. At 8.30 the next day I had the take from hell. It was so fast my reel handle was almost impossible to grab. That fish ran from forty yards in front of the dugouts to the other end and only stopped because it ran out of lake. It had to be the Parrot. In its wisdom the carp kited to my right, disappeared behind the island and straightened the hook. My friend Sam Fox caught the Parrot and it did exactly the same to him, only he swam after it.

I could get takes in daylight but had never had one at night. In the end I gave up night fishing the Copse and moved over to the match lake for the nights, returning the next day. To be honest, I found the match lake relatively easy. I just used to plop it out in a swim I fancied and it would often go off – there was no science or understanding to it at all. I think it was a combination of good bait and pure luck.

Some weeks later I found the two biggies along with three other twenties in the Back Bay by the twig island. I watched them for a while and luckily the three smaller fish mooched further up the bay leaving the two big girls on their own. One bait was cast to a small clean patch to the right of the teabag swim while with the other rod I managed to land a freelined floater cake a couple of feet in front of the carp. (The cake was made by doubling the amount of eggs so the mix was really runny and then baked in the oven.) Up came the Parrot, slurped down the floater and whack! I totally missed it and the hook ended up in the tree above my head. I think I might have struck too hard. The Pineapple didn't spook but just waddled off, came across my bottom bait and ate it. To cut a long story short, after a five-minute battle the hook slipped. I couldn't believe it – I had lost and missed the two biggest carp I had ever seen in my life in the space of less than a minute. I packed up and I went to the match lake. Luckily I caught a 24lb 12oz mirror (the old fish) that night but it still didn't make up for the disaster of the day before.

I met up with the pineapple once again one dinnertime (unfortunately mine, not hers). I was stalking around the little gravel mounds when a fish slowly cruised past. It was no more than twelve feet from where I was wading. This fish was huge. I didn't even attempt to cast at it, as I knew it was too big for me to even try to land. It felt like trying to shoot an elephant with a pea-shooter. I spent a lot of time up the trees just watching. When a pattern started to emerge I tried to be one jump ahead setting the traps just before the fish arrived. This is exactly what happened on our final encounter. I hooked her over a twenty-bait patch in a shallow gully. She just swam very slowly and determinedly out into the middle of the lake, where she just stopped. After what must have been around a minute or so the rod started to buck: we were on the move again. My line broke.

In hindsight I think the Pineapple was spawn bound, and she certainly seemed to be bigger every time I saw her. She was a very distinctive fish due to her colour. Pete saw her, Sam saw her and I believe Mr McDonald saw her. As far I know she was never caught.

SHORT AND SWEET

Short sessions are my favourites. Short sessions are without doubt very productive.

The result of a six-hour session.

This trip lasted a whole eleven hours.

When you've only a few hours to catch one, you make damn sure you are on them, and if you do get on the fish you don't mess it up and spook them with clumsy angling. On lower stocked lakes, say with two carp per acre, I'm more than happy spending an hour of my short stay just looking. If carp can't be found you just have to call on your experience and guess.

The first good thing about these short day trips (and there are many) is that you're not there long enough to lose your confidence or become despondent, so you're always on top of your game, able to watch the water nearly one hundred percent of the time. Find them and you can catch them.

The second good point is that you don't need a bed chair, bivvy, bivvy table, television and Jacuzzi, so you can carry the bare minimum and up sticks if need be in minutes. It's strange, but each time I set up again in a new swim my confidence returns.

Jed and I had a job on our hands overlooking this lake. What's the record for a carp caught off a scaffold?

The third plus point is that if you arrive at, say, midday on pressured water you can see which areas have received all the pressure during the period prior to your arrival. If you wander off to the area receiving the least or no angling pressure, lo and behold there they are, loads of carp. They certainly like escaping the bombardment.

I find determining the right baiting level is very critical for this type of semi-stalking. You need just enough to get them having a look. Sometimes it's half a pouch of pellet and a small bag containing your bait and a few bits, at other times I go mad and will put in fifty baits and a bag. When boilie fishing, I do like to have around twenty baits out there and top up if I catch a bream or something. If you're moving perhaps every hour, these little pockets of bait will be found dotted around the lake, a nice way to establish bait.

Short sessions are very intense, but personally I'm sure I can catch more in eight four-hour sessions than in one thirty-two-hour trip. This won't apply to all anglers, as no doubt there are many good long-session anglers out there, but I can only speak for myself and I'm a rubbish night angler. Kev Woodrow reckons I'm scared of the dark.

Even on a large pit, short sessions teach you an awful lot about the place in a short space of time, simply because you'll be fishing a lot of different swims rather than sitting in one forever. Interesting areas will soon become apparent. Best of all, when you blank you can tell yourself, 'Oh well, I only went for a few hours, what do you expect?' It's great, you can blank and not be bothered.

Lucky Old Sod

The bait group used to bait every lake in Kent, or so it seemed, with baits sorted by Steve. My job was to bait Sundridge Lake. During the close season I drove forty miles to the lake twice a week to get in my quota of baits, probably about 500 hand-rolled proteins each time. It was 16 June, and bang: they loved it. The carp were a tad on the small side, and during the next month I caught something like seventy fish with only a handful being doubles.

Time to get on the phone: 'Steve, I'm bored of all these little ones, any ideas where I can catch a biggie?' 'Johnson's Railway Lake has been baited – it's hard but there is fish to 28lb-plus,' came the reply. That's big enough for me, so off I went.

First impressions were scary. The Railway was a great big oblong pit, as deep as you like, gin clear and full of weed plus a couple of cars (I thought I had found a bar once, but it turned out to be the bonnet of a mini traveller). Fishing the road bank was another angler, and it's a good starting point to talk to the locals. 'Any good mate?' I shouted into his bivvy; I say bivvy, but it was in fact a London taxi. Apparently he had fished it on and off for four years without a fish. I didn't have a clue where to start. On the Railway bank there was a long piece of margin with no swims in it, just reeds lining the bank, which looked carpy enough. I tied a few willow branches back in a spot at the end of the reeds and had just enough room to set up. One rod went straight out about a rod length and a half and the other twenty yards down the margin to my left. The near rod was baited with forty or so baits on a clean spot, while the other was a single pop-up three inches off the lead over some thin silkweed.

After an hour I landed a 7lb tench from the baited patch. Out went a bit more bait and along came another tench. By 6am the next morning I had landed five PB tench up to 8lb 2oz – result. I knew the bait, rig and swim was spot on and I'm always happy catching a few tench. It tells me my rigs and bait are OK. At last I had a bite on the left-hand pop-up. It was a twitchy sort of take but surprisingly there was a carp on the end. To my relief, it didn't fight much and was soon netted. I couldn't believe my eyes – twelve hours on the lake and I had bagged one of the biggest. I ran round to the taxi driver to do the camera honours. He couldn't believe it either.

Was it luck or getting it right? Luck, I think. Catching carp from hard waters may not be luck but getting the big one first fish I think just may be. I never returned.

The next year I was lucky again. My friend Mark from Bromley got me a ticket for Cotton Farm at Dartford. I gave him a recipe and he baited it for the both of us. The bait was a milk protein flavoured with

Fish caught on a single pop-up bait in 1985 – early trials at Cotton Farm.

violet oil. I arrived for my first session during the second week of the season. My plan was to fish over a lot of bait and wait for them to come to me. I walked up to the lake to find one other angler, who happened to be in an area I fancied. We had a chat and it emerged he had blanked for four days. Now, for some reason I thought Cotton was an easy doubles water, but maybe not. The kind chap helped me carry my gear to the other end of the lake. On the way I saw a couple of carp in the long finger bay, so out came a fly rod and in seconds an 8lb common took my slow sinking flake. Good start, I had a fish before even getting to my swim. Two days and one tench later, it was obvious my plan wasn't working so a move was called for. I had been seeing a few carp in the margin of a small cliff at the mouth of the long bay but hadn't thought it was enough to move off my baited patch. Shame I didn't move earlier.

A single pop-up was cast to the fish but no freebies, as I didn't want to spook them. The other rod went in another area over a little bit of bait. An hour later the pop-up was away and I was attached to a long-looking, possible mid-twenty. The scale reading made my legs wobble, 30lb 8oz, my first thirty, and to be honest a bit of a shock. In the past I thought I might be in with a chance of a big one but this was out of the blue. I had a 19lb 6oz a couple of hours later and then went home. I never returned, as I'd again caught the biggest fish on the first trip. Another lucky one.

I think it's strange that sometimes carp fishing can seem so easy but at other times you work your socks off for very little return. It's probably down to the law of averages. Go fishing enough and some days you will get it right. Most days we don't.

After any blank session I come away knowing I got it wrong, not blaming the

Still catching them on a single pop-up in 2005.

weather or the fish not having it, or whatever. I know they didn't have what I offered or I simply offered it in the wrong place. I always like to learn something from a blank even if it's only not to fish those spots in those conditions again. The process of elimination will lead you to some good areas. After catching that thirty in 1985 my personal fishing changed. I had reached my goal and I no longer cared if I was catching much or not – well I say that, but time was no longer something I had spare. My two sons, Jed and Olli, were born in 1986 and 1988 and all my milk powders were consumed by them! After their mother departed, leaving me to bring the

boys up on my own, I had to pack up carp fishing or take them with me, so along they came. This led me to the pressured day-ticket waters.

Rigs

Whenever you read any of the carp magazines you will find little pictures under the heading of rigs. Usually a new super rig is nothing more than an alternative way of attaching the bait via the hair, or a method of attaching the lead. It's all about the last few feet of your tackle. Personally, my rig starts at the reel and ends at the bait. The whole picture is far more important than

Graham about to release a beautiful fish. 8lb line, 1¼ TC rods, size 10 hook.

just the so-called business end. Surely the use of a heavy backlead will change the dynamics of the whole rig and the same applies to all permutations, for example, using different weight bobbins, hook gauges and so on.

My thoughts have always been that the bait most likely to be picked up is the one without a hook or line attached, so the nearer we can get to this the better. To achieve this aim I have always adopted a light tackle approach. Not all carp live in

141

'I think the rig's working, don't you, Olli?'

any more than the rig that preceded it. A very simple hair-rig again fits with the rig camo theme. I see it as a contradiction to camo the leads and tubing and then use a hooking arrangement covered with various rings and bits of plastic. These complicated hook arrangements must stand out like a sore thumb. I don't know what a carp can actually see in clear water but I know what I can see.

When the hair first arrived on the scene it was unbelievable and we all caught fish, but then someone would show you something new and we all slowly moved from rig to rig still catching a few carp along the way. The interesting thing is, I didn't stop catching on the standard hair, but just moved on because of fashion. The only real progress came with Rob Maylin's bent hook and it is basically used by everyone today, including me, via the knotless knot.

Back to the whole picture again, I like to use slack line and a very light bobbin. You won't find a backlead in my box because these give you a tight line. It may lie along the lake bed but it is basically still tight. If a carp bumps into a slack line it simple rides up over its body, and a light bobbin does not impede this. It can be no different to the carp than swimming through weed. A tight line, however, must be a very different story. The moment the bobbin is clipped on your line it will stop sinking, so I often leave it for ten minutes to settle before clipping on the bobbin. If fishing ten yards or less I rarely use a bobbin at all. I see a slack line as being as crucial a part of carp fishing as the ground baiting pattern. It's all about the bigger picture.

The main tweaking of the rig I go in for is only altering the length of the hooklength or the length of the hair. As for hooklength materials, whatever is on my reel is used for the hooklength too. Depending on where I'm fishing, it's mono

snag-infested lakes. Rig camouflage is all the rage at the moment, and the light tackle fits well within this school of thought. Eight-pound line must be less visible than fifteen, and a fine wire size ten is surely harder to detect than a heavyweight size four hook.

Over the years I have been influenced by the new secret rig whispers just the same as most of us but they have never caught me between five and fifteen pounds. The hair is always 1.7 mono. This fine hair gives natural movement and using it at least an inch and a quarter long allows bait and hook separation to do the business if the bait is spat out.

Above all, the rig must deliver and present a bait to where the carp are feeding. It's no good using a rig that blasts through weed if the fish are feeding on top of it and vice versa. This is obvious really but is surprisingly often overlooked. Balanced baits? Well I used to balance all of my baits but now I only balance them in winter or when using very light hookbaits, such as particles or very small boillies. I don't think carp can detect the weight of a small hook when attached to a large boilie but there's no doubt they can detect the hook weight when attached to a piece of corn.

One rig I have been using recently is the no pop-up, pop-up rig. It's simply a shot two inches from the hook but used with a bottom bait. The theory is that the weight of the shot helps turn the hook as well as pinning down the hooklength. I've caught fish on it but unless I try it on a runs water it's difficult to draw any firm conclusions.

Pop-ups are different. I actually use one of the fancy hooklength materials, mantis in fact. The hair is kept short using a peeled-back section set up with a knotless knot. The actual knot is used with the outer coating still intact and the only piece of the hook length that is peeled back is the pivot point where the counterbalance sits. Even the knot attaching the hook length to the swivel is kept solid. This way (and the same applies to bottom baits) the bait does not fold back on itself and lie alongside the anti-tangle tubing. Hence I don't use swivels with a ring attached. It must be better for the bait to be pushed away from the rest of the terminal tackle.

It's all very simple. If you give them a bait they really want, you will catch on almost any half-sensible rig. After thirty years of carp fishing these are my rig conclusions. I'm not saying I'm right but it works for me. The best rig is the one you have the most confidence in; it's good to arrive at a point where rigs and bait are forgotten about so you can concentrate on the more important issue of chucking it where the carp want it.

Day-ticket Waters

The handy thing about day-ticket waters is that they are very busy and noisy, very useful when you have two young children in tow. Jed and Olli's noise blended in with the rest so they didn't become a problem. So what makes small, often well-stocked lakes tricky? It's purely down to angling pressure. The higher the standard of angling the harder the lakes become. Carp are encountering rigs and baits constantly, unlike their counterparts in vast, under-stocked lakes. These pressured fish can probably learn in a year what could take ten years for the carp in low-stocked waters to learn.

On any pressured lake there will be a trend, a method that the majority of anglers are using. In a nutshell, clock what's being done and do the opposite. The beauty of fishing these heavily stocked waters is that they respond very quickly to a winning method. Often one day with a new tactic will tell you if you got it right or wrong. Quality bait will always help but even more so on lakes where a lot of cheap, inferior baits are the norm. At the time (mid 1990s), Iden Wood in Kent and Cobbleacre in Norfolk fell into this category. The local lads were using all the right label tackle but skimped on bait. The boys and I arrived at Cobbleacre with two thousand oiled-up fishmeals. The bailiff at the time turned up and asked the obvious while looking at my bag of bait. 'Is that

Pressured waters contain some mighty fine fish, such as this beautiful common.

your bait mate?' 'Yep.' 'You won't do any good on that, only red or yellows will do good here.' That night no one had a take apart from us. We had eleven. Our bait was new and different and boy, did they like it.

We had similar results on a day-ticket water near Frant. Two or three fish were being caught a day in the stumps lake. We used 12mm boilies as opposed to 15 or 18mm and fished over a hundred baits, topping up with twenty five after each take. The best we managed was twenty-six takes in a day. It's amazing the difference a good bait can make. Iden Wood was similar but a tad trickier. Fishing the obvious spots, like the island, as everyone did, produced a few but the small ones. The big fish were more in the open water. We started by fishing the near neglected margins as everyone fished the far bank. On our first night I had a mid-double on Jed's rod. He had the right hump with me but I honestly did think it

was a tench. The next take was his, whosever rod it was on. I was using a bag with forty 12mm boillies inside just to offer what was at the time a very different baiting approach. An hour later I was forgiven for catching the double. My rod was away and ten-year-old Jed landed his first twenty. During the period we fished Iden Wood it was receiving a lot of bait and we unlocked it by using a one-bait stringer. This rig can be a real winner on the right lake. I think the carp suck both baits in at once, so, with the stringer bait acting as a freebie, the carp take both baits with confidence.

If you're fishing small, high-stocked lakes and you're not catching, you've got it wrong, it's as simple as that. Just keep ringing the changes until it happens. The answer can sometimes be as simple as a shorter hooklength or dumping the heavy bobbins and backleads for slack line and light bobbins. Just be different.

Over the years I've played about a lot with light line fishing, and as I've said before, the best bait is the one with no line or hook attached, so the closer we can get to this the better – light line and small hooks. When using light line I can see no point in just using a light hooklength as you still have thick line going through the swim, so I fish light all the way through. Now, landing big carp on light line is very dependent on your rods. I have two fly blanks made up as carp rods for this very purpose. They are so soft they really balance out the tackle, and carp can be played almost the same as on conventional heavier gear. If I put my hook into something solid and pull as hard as possible, the rods keep bending and I can't break 5lb line. The advantage of light gear is that you can use a very fine light hook, like Kamasan Animals. The thinner the hook the easier it goes in and hookbaits act more naturally as the hook is so much lighter. Another plus is that a light lead is enough to pull the hook home, so you can cast near fish with less chance of spooking them. Don't get me wrong – if I'm fishing a weedy or snaggy pit I will be using a 15lb outfit, but given the choice I'd fish as light as I can get away with.

When fishing pressured waters I normally have different options on each rod. If I find a going method I use that on one rod and mess about with the other, looking for another winning combination. Short term it may cost me a few takes but long term it will put more fish on the bank. In the grander scheme of things a lot of little tricks can be discovered and stored in the carp tactics section of my little brain to be called upon at any time or on any other lake that I might fish. I used to fish an estate lake in Sussex and over the years I had caught all the carp, so I used it for rig and bait testing. In the very early 1980s Steve introduced me to tiger nuts. The first

time the lake ever saw them the carp went berserk, and we had loads of takes. I fished them one more short evening and had fish again; after that I dropped the bait and told Pete. Once I found a method that was working I saw no point in catching the same fish all over again. The bait and rig was saved for another lake in the future and I started looking for an alternative way to catch them. At the end of the day carp are carp whatever lake they are swimming in and an effective method will be equally useful on any other carp lake.

One thing I find very important on any water is considering what effect each rod has on the other. I never put two rods in more or less the same spot. If carp are using a small island you only need one rod on it. Another rod only gets in the way and the extra line in the swim may be enough to put them on edge. I prefer to hedge my bets. The baits will be well apart and, more importantly, my lines will not be cutting each other off.

On large, low-stocked pits I don't really get too tactical. The problem here is that

I needed two barrows, one for my gear and one for Olli.

145

A 27lb Leney common, say no more.

you are often not on fish. It's that simple. No wonder rig or tactic will catch them if they are not there. A good food bait and your favourite tried and tested rig is enough. As soon as doubt about what you're doing creeps in, you will end up chasing your own tail. The best bait and rig in the world is one you are confident in so you can forget about them and worry about casting in the right place at the right time.

THE TWILIGHT ZONE

By now you must have realized how I rate confidence as a top carp catcher. A positive outlook will always catch more carp than the negative. Why is this? At the end of the day your bait is in the water just the same, regardless of your mental approach. The difference is that when you are on a roll the rods keep going off. Jack Hilton used to write about having 'that feeling' when he just knew it was going to happen and invariably it did. So is it a chicken and egg scenario? Do we somehow transfer our thoughts to the carp and make it happen or would we have had a take regardless?

Years ago I was plugged into the local grapevine and knew what was going on at the local carp lakes. There were times when the going got tough and very few carp were coming out. I think a lot of anglers were beaten before they even arrived at the lake.

Armed with the knowledge that the fishing was really slow they approached it with a negative, 'well, you never know' attitude. The more anglers with a negative approach the greater the negative collective. It was at these times I always had my best hits. I felt that if very few carp had been caught then they must be up for a right pasting. Whatever the reason for my success during these periods, it happened too many times to be just coincidence.

I've had similar sessions when the opposite has happened. I could be happily fishing away with maybe a carp or two under my belt when Pete would arrive. Now Pete was very successful on this particular lake with methods that I wouldn't have dreamed of using. If he turned up and had a carp fairly soon my confidence in my approach was blown away, and I knew I wouldn't have another take. I might as well have gone home there and then. Again, this happened too many times to be just coincidence. It sounds mad, but my approach just seemed to stop working as soon as Pete arrived. Pete wasn't the problem, it was all in my head, but in my head or not, the reality was I stopped catching.

Sixth sense is sometimes spoken about in carp-angling circles, and without a doubt if you are lucky enough to have it you're laughing. It's when for some unknown reason you just know where to cast. I have a totally daft method that has caught me a lot of fish over the years, almost too daft to mention. I told Nigel Sharpe about it and he just gave me a funny look. I can be fishing a huge pit, acres of open water in front of me, wondering where to cast. I look out and if I see something like a feather or a single floating leaf out in the lake I land my bait right next to it. I'm fully aware of how crazy this sounds, but I have caught loads by doing it. Maybe I'm just lucky, who knows. I just regard it as the carp gods giving me a sign.

By now you may be thinking what planet is this bloke on, but I bet a lot of you have a lucky hat or a lucky jacket that you daren't wash just in case you wash out its magic. It's all superstition but in varying degrees.

During my thirty years of carp fishing I've come across some very good carp catchers. After a while of knowing them you got to see why they were so good. Steve always had fantastic bait and rigs. Kev could tell you he was fishing in ten feet, three and a half inches of water over a sandy bottom next to a patch of silkweed. Sam would swim out and hand place rigs, and so on. It's quite easy to see why these guys are good at what they do, but then along comes somebody who seems to get it all wrong yet catches loads. Kerry was such an angler. He was a very good sea angler but when carp fishing he seriously lacked finesse. He would turn up with any old bait and rig, lob it out willy-nilly and still catch loads. He was a human fish magnet. I'm pretty sure if he used his Zipplex with a breakaway lead and lugworm he would still catch more carp than most. Maybe Kerry thought that if he could catch fish from a huge lake like the sea then a small pond would be a doddle. Who knows!

Sometimes there is rhyme or reason to our results. A couple of years ago in the spring I was on a roll. No new super bait or rig, I just couldn't put a foot wrong. Everywhere I went the carp would oblige. I caught two twenties in an afternoon session from a lake that held only two twenties. I fished a morning on a small water that contained only three carp and had a twenty-three-pounder. First night on Camelot and I caught the silver common. Next a day-ticket lake for a twelve-hour session, one bite and the biggest carp in the lake graced my net. On Swangey Lake for a seven-hour session I caught six carp. I could go on. It was a mad period – thought I was Kevin Maddocks for a while. Then, bang, back down to earth and I went twelve days without a bite. I remember thinking to myself, 'am I ever going to get another bite?' Minutes later the reel was spinning and I actually hooked a carp at last. Not for long though, as it slipped the hook. Six trips later I managed to actually hook another, only to be cut off on some mussels. For some reason I had gone from being Kevin Maddocks to Mr Bean.

I think the explanation was that after a couple of blanks my confidence took a nosedive and went further downhill with every blank. I couldn't catch a cold. Luckily for me I had a fantastic December and things went back to normal. During that run-less period I hadn't made any drastic changes. Maybe I should have, who knows, but I do know that when your confidence is low, so are your catch returns.

Rod Hutchinson used to say 'chuck 'em out and read a book or something', anything to distract your thoughts from your traps, as if trying to pretend that you're not really fishing for them. He believed in his mental approach and it worked for him. Chris Yates is a very spiritual angler, and who can argue with his results. I remember in the late 1970s Pete was sitting in the pub one dinner time when he had the urge to get to the lake. He just knew something was going to happen, and it did. Two big carp from a tricky water on a short afternoon trip. On another trip with Pete to an eighty-acre, low-stock pit, I had a premonition that I would catch a particular carp the next morning, and I did. Spooky, isn't it?

There is a very fine line between success and failure in carp fishing. Exactly what the line is I really don't know, it's very hard to define. Some anglers simply have 'the knack'. So can any conclusions be gained from these ramblings? Probably not. Now over to my son, Jed.

JED'S STORY

It was Sunday night as I was packing away on a busy day-ticket water, thinking to myself I wish I could fish a nice, quiet lake for a change. The crowds and the rat race were getting to me big time. This isn't what angling is about for me – so what if the lake contains some big fish, I was not enjoying myself anymore. So on the way home I thought that I might as well pop in to see my mate Kev. Whilst excitedly chatting away about our main passion in life – angling – he hands me his photo album. Each fish is more impressive than the last, until I arrive at a gorgeous proper English carp. I gazed upon this magnificent creature totally slack-jawed. Kev laughed and said, 'Stunning, isn't she?'. I just nodded my head for I was so blown away by the long, old-looking linear. When I could finally manage a few words I didn't bother to ask its weight, for this great fish should not be reduced to a mere number (nor should any carp for that matter). 'Kev, mate, where does this carp live? I have just got to find out,' I said. He just smiled and said I'll take you there and show you next weekend. The words just rang in my ears I could think of nothing else all the way home or the whole week at work. For here was my chance to see where my new obsession lived.

So when the weekend finally came, as usual when I'm excited about fishing I woke up before my alarm. I thought to myself, I must be keen, I hate getting up early, especially on Saturday. But today was no ordinary day, it was the day that Kev was going to take me into another world, a world where my dream lived. So, as you could imagine, I was absolutely buzzing big time on the way to Kev's house, I simply couldn't wait to see this lake. When I knocked on his door I was like a kid at

Mine at last!

Christmas, though I tried as best I could to hide my excitement and to look cool and act like a real pro (yeah, right). As we pulled into the car park I simply couldn't wait to get to the banks of the lake. I reckon Kev could tell how excited I was because whenever he looked at me he laughed to himself.

The view from the car park provided me with a sight of a small, attractive, tree-lined gravel pit with sets of lily pads at either end of the lake. The first swim we arrived at was the steep, gravel-sided car park swim, which offered a great view of the gin-clear lake. While Kev kindly showed me all the carpy looking swims around the lake and even told me about the depths and features, which was much appreciated, I simply couldn't wait to wet a line. So I planned my assault for the very next weekend for a Saturday till Sunday night job.

When Friday night eventually came I decided to take no chances and re-spool with brand new 12lb line as the lake is heavily tree-lined and filled with lily pads. As usual, I lovingly hand-rolled my bait, which was my own blend of fishmeals and birdfoods, a bait I had great confidence in. I was on the road by five, as it was late March and not light till about six. At half past five I pulled into the car park with just a few cars in evidence and thought it's lucky the lake's not busy. To my amazement there was only one other tench angler on the lake.

I opted to fish the big sandy swim, for it covered most of the deep, open water which I thought would be a good place to start because it was still quite cold and you could see the whole lake from this swim. Drawing on all my years of angling know-how, I just lobbed two baits out in the

149

Jed with an ancient old carp from Norfolk.

middle, making sure I felt the lead down (that's a must) and putting a bit of bait round them both. Then I just got the rest of my tackle sorted and sat back on my chair (rods out first – also a must), surveying the lake, when I had a screamer of a take. I jumped a mile and nearly fell over, I was in such shock, as I hadn't been there long. I struck the screaming rod, which nicely hooped over; 'carp on' was my first thought, with my heart pounding away. It was not until I felt the tell-tale taps of a tench on the end that I could calm down, so without hiccups I netted what was a fine specimen of probably about seven to eight pounds. Nice one, I thought, I don't mind catching a few of these. How wrong could I get – I ended up catching half a dozen of the red-eyed demons, all of similar size to the first, which was not bad for my first ever session.

It was now 17 April, my birthday, and I had blanked so far carp-wise, although I had caught loads of tench. I couldn't believe how many were in there, and of such a good stamp. But bearing in mind there were only four known carp in about two to three acres and obviously hundreds of tench, I knew I was up against it from the start (love it). In the past my birthday sessions have produced the goods carp-wise, so I was well up for it, as you can imagine. It was a hot, sunny day – good carp-watching weather – and on my second lap of the lake climbing all the trees I finally spotted my obsession. I was thirty feet up a tree on the point and right below me were two carp. One was a mirror, about mid-double, and the other was Friendly, for sure. I knew this because of its sheer size and bulk and the light colour that Kev told me about. I wasn't ready for the sight of Friendly, it just blew me away. I just had to catch it now, no matter how long it took, I was that well and truly hooked.

Friendly was patrolling the area that I later found out was her favourite spot for sunbathing. It was off a tree-lined bank with no swims as such along it; off the end of the trees the water was about twelve feet deep rising sharply up the gravel shelf to the bank. It was so frustrating. I tried everything: baiting the gravel slopes, floaters, zig-rigs and float-fishing on the drop for it, but nothing worked. Before I knew it, dark was upon me, so I decided to set some traps as near to the treeline as possible. The night just brought tench after tench and an eighteen-egg mix was soon ravenously eaten.

The day was the same as the day before, just chasing shadows. In fact, the rest of the summer was the same, which was maddening. I only came close to catching it once. I had my normal baited spots along the tree on the gravel, and after looking for the carp I finally found the mid-double mirror on my baited spot. I quickly lowered down a rig with a double 14mm bait on it (supposedly tench-proof). With the aid of my Polaroid glasses (also a must-have item) I was shocked to see the carp had done me, he had picked up and spat out my bait. So I quickly set up a rig

with a single bait on and was just about to lower it back in because the coast was clear, when suddenly I spotted Friendly coming straight for the spot. Shaking like a leaf, I lowered my rig and held the line down on the bottom with my rod still in my hand. At this point Friendly was about a foot away from my bait; then, to my total horror, it went down on my bait, but just as it was about to suck my hook-bait up, it spooked. Gutted was a total understatement.

It was now late summer so I made up a plan to move off and come back in the winter, when hopefully the tench would be asleep. My first day trip back was in late December and the lake was basically frozen over, so nothing was seen or caught. My first night, a few weeks later, was a complete blank, but the good thing was I got a few liners twenty yards out in the deep water on a narrow gravel seam near some silkweed. I baited the spot with the rest of my six-egg mix ready for next week. The next Saturday, 14 January, I was just about to leave the house when the phone rang. It was my old school mate Thomas Adams from Hastings, whom I happened to be with when I caught my first 30lb common from Camelot (my lucky charm, or so I thought).

I finally got to the lake about two, and got my baits out first. One was on a home-made yellow pop-up, and the other was a balanced bottom bait over seventeen free-bies on the gravel spot. It was nearly dark now, so I recast both rods and put another five baits out over the bottom bait rod. I awoke at about 1am to a single bleep on the bottom bait rod and thought it was Friendly's tail just hitting the slack line. I must have nodded back off because the next thing I knew I had a very slow take on the bottom bait. As I struck it, I got that satisfying feeling of a bent rod and a slow, very heavy weight on the end. After only thirty seconds I flicked on my headlamp as it neared the net, then wished I hadn't because I saw Friendly just out of reach of the net. But the carp gods smiled on me: I netted it first time. I had finally lived out my dream. The emotions running through me I simply cannot describe, 'thrilled' would be an understatement. I phoned my dad at about half past one in the morning, and he could hardly understand a word I was saying because I spoke so fast. I badly wanted good pictures, so I reluctantly sacked the fish up. I got totally soaked in the process, but what did I care – I had just caught my obsession. I really couldn't sleep that night or feel the cold, I was just buzzing. So when dad and Kev kindly arrived in the morning I was still shaking, but thanks to them I got some great photos and when Friendly swam off strongly to fight another day I punched the air for joy.

CONCLUSION

Well, I'm coming to a close now, so it's time maybe to reflect. On the low-stocked waters, location is the key. The fewer fish you have per acre the more important location becomes. If you have twenty carp in twenty acres they could all be in the same quarter of an acre, leaving the remaining nineteen and three quarter acres totally barren. I've stuck to simple but effective rigs and have always taken a lot of care over my bait. My tackle has often been a right old mismatch but my bait the best I can afford. The answer to low-stock waters is never about changing your stick or bag mix. Stay with your favourite rigs, bait and just make sure you get on them.

On the pressured waters, ring the changes. I don't mean try a new bait each new season, I mean ring the changes every session or every few hours. You will soon know when you have got it right. Be different from everybody else. Fish different areas, different-sized bait, long hooklengths, short ones, try heavy baiting, single baits – the list is endless. If you find something that works for you, don't change it for the latest rig or whatever you've read about. It's all about confidence in what you're doing. The bottom line is: on the pressured waters you have to fool them, while on the low-stocked pits you have to find them.

My preference is to fish low-stock, quiet waters. I like to be away from the crowds, fishing for unnamed and old original carp. They are not all monsters, but a 12lb carp doesn't know it's only 12lb. If you enjoy fishing runs waters or lakes full of imported carp, however, then go ahead and do it. The bottom line is that we enjoy ourselves. It's important not to take yourself too seriously, and if you catch a fish that makes your day then please smile for the camera. Looking back over the last thirty years of carp fishing, a lot has changed. Tackle is far better, carp are bigger and more plentiful but angling is still angling and the fundamentals remain the same. Watercraft cannot be bought, nor can original thinking. If you want to be successful you can lay siege and bore them out or you can go your own way and try to catch them on your own terms. At the end of the day it doesn't really matter, it's only fishing. Just as you think you've got it sussed something or someone comes along and blows all your theories to bits. But that's what makes it interesting.

Big thanks to the legend that is Bob Church for inviting me to write this chapter and thanks also to all my angling friends especially Pete, Roy, Steve, Alan, Jed, Kev and my two little boys Jed and Olli. Tight lines and broken scale springs.

ABOVE: J.D. and a beauty from a little-fished pit.

RIGHT: Rockabilly Roy Turner: thirty years a carper and at last he's got the hang of it.

5. Carping My Way

by Des Taylor

It's funny how you end up being put into a character box – in my case 'Mr Controversial' – and yet when it comes to catching fish I would back myself against anyone. I'm not best known as a carp angler but I can tell you that my buzzers sound off enough to keep me happy. This is an unusual statement for me because rarely do I blow my own trumpet, but I have become more than a little fed up with my fish catches being overshadowed by my forthright views. In this article I am not going to be controversial in the least. I won't be talking about cormorants, the Environment Agency or any political subject – what I will be talking about is catching carp my way.

THE BASICS

To catch carp consistently you have to understand the species you are trying to catch. Too often an angler buys all the right gear and bait but in reality he knows very little about the animal he is trying to hunt down. If you were trying to track any other wild creature you would want to know where it lives, what it likes to do in the day and at night. When will it be on the bottom

A truly awesome-looking common.

To the dinner table with a bait boat. There is no better presentation than that given by a bait boat.

of the lake and when will it be up in the water? What does it like to eat? What scares it to death? Does it spend more time in one area of a lake than another? The more you can find out about the carp the better carp angler you will be.

I'm afraid there are no shortcuts to this information but it does come easier if you read articles by good anglers who have been around for a few years and caught carp from a number of waters (not 'legends in their own lunchbox') and have caught the same fish time and again from the same water. Go to carp shows where all the experts are on show, ask them questions about carp rather than what reel to buy and what camouflage coat to wear. Those issues are important but not as important as understanding the carp itself.

I remember reading Dick Walker years ago and in his own words he said that he was an unsuccessful pike angler because he didn't understand the species and could never think like a pike. He understood

carp, could think like them and so ended up catching the British record – that's how important it is to understand the fish itself.

DINNER TABLES AND HOT SPOTS

These are the most important areas in the lake, yet some anglers never find them and again never understand them. Carp, especially big carp, don't eat everywhere, even if you throw huge amounts of bait in. On the other hand, there will be areas in a lake where carp will always be tempted to feed, no matter how many times they have been caught there, and these areas I call the 'dinner table'. In their lifetime, carp will almost certainly check out every inch of the lake and that's from the bottom to the surface, in twenty feet of water or just inches and I'm talking about fish from four pounds to forty. Carp are the most curious of fish and this will see them searching

155

everywhere, but they will only actually eat in certain places, at least on a regular basis. On clear waters with low stocking levels of carp you can spot areas that have been 'hoovered' clean; even the stones are shining as they have been in the carp's mouth or rubbed together as the fish has moved about in the area searching for natural food or an angler's bait. These are 'dinner tables' and you must have a bait there.

Note that I said bait, not baits. For some reason it's a common thought that your chances are improved if you get more rods in a good area but I believe the opposite! Let me give an example of this. One of the best carp anglers I have ever seen, Wayne I n, was fishing the shallows on the bottom lake at Acton Burnell, a water known difficult. Wayne had found a dinner table in the shallows and noticed that every few hours a small group of big carp would come in there and feed for ten minutes and then leave.

This was nothing unusual, many syndicate members had seen this but catching them was a different thing! Wayne had noticed that in the past once anglers had placed their allowed three rods in the area, the carp disappeared and avoided the area when rigs were placed. He waited for the fish to leave, then placed only one rod in the whole area – probably one acre of water. He fished one rod only for 48 hours with his other two rods still in the holdall. If memory serves me well he took four carp all over 30lb, the best over 40lb, proof enough that one rod on the dinner table is better than three or four!

Many of the dinner tables I have found are fewer than three yards from the bank,

A 30lb common from the dinner table, off the snag above my right-hand shoulder in the photo.

especially on lightly fished waters. Popular spots are under trees, near snags, next to a weed bed or under a high tree near the water's edge even if the branches don't spread over the water, or next to a pole or post that has been placed in the water. I remember fishing the mighty St Cassien in southern France, a huge water where most anglers would boat their baits out to great distance. Yet near 'Ellis Point' I spotted a steel pole in the water on a gravel bar in two feet of water only two yards from the bank. In a couple of days of having a bait there I took a couple of fish to mid-thirties. I think carp like eating the naturals that cling to such structures and they also like to brush themselves against them.

The chances are you are fishing a water that is like a mud bath because there are a good few carp in there and it's heavily fished. The good news is even though you cannot see the dinner tables, at least with the water this colour you know the carp are feeding well. To find dinner tables on such waters is different but not difficult. Look for 'bubblers', which are fish that are sending bubbles up to the surface. This is a good sign, but I'm afraid doesn't guarantee success. Bubbling carp can be feeding heavily on natural food such as blood-worm, nymphs and snails and it is very difficult to catch these fish on conventional baits such as boilies. The other thing is that lots of bubbles may not be from carp at all. Every species, even pike and eels, send up bubbles, some of them looking exactly like carp bubbles, so beware. Even in coloured waters there will be areas that are more coloured than the rest and this usually means either carp or, at worst, a shoal of bream are feeding heavily in the area: fish it straight away!

There will be swims on such hard-fished waters that consistently produce big carp. Anglers have realized this and so the bait keeps going in there. These will be good

swims forever and a day, so make sure you find them. The problem with such hard-fished swims is that your preparation, in terms of rigs, bait and tackle, has to be better than the other anglers', which we will talk about later in this chapter. Carp are only another fish and in some situations are easy to catch but on hard-fished waters where the big fish have been caught a number of times you really do have to look for an edge.

From dinner tables I will now move on to hot spots, which very often are the same area but require a different approach to catch the carp. Let me explain. A dinner table is an area where carp feed on the bottom of the lake but unfortunately they spend very little of their lives on the bottom which is why we spend so much fishing the bottom without a take! It is a misconception that carp spend most of their time grubbing around on the bottom – believe me they don't, they spend most of their time roaming about, or even suspended doing nothing in mid-water. When carp are doing this and you have your bait on the bottom you catch nothing. This is a hot spot but you have to approach it a different way, that is, with a bait fished off the bottom. Again, we will talk of this later. At this point I cannot stress enough that by only fishing baits hard on the bottom, or pop-ups and snowmen only inches from the bottom, you are missing out on a lot of fish.

With three or four rods, don't forget to experiment with a bait fished at various levels. I remember fishing in the next peg to one of the all-time great carp anglers, Kevin Maddocks. I was fishing three rods hard on the bottom and had not a take. Kevin, fishing the same area, fished over six feet of water and had zig-rigs fished two feet, three feet and five feet from the bottom. He took three 30lb+ carp in two hours, while I blanked. By the time I had changed my rigs the chance had gone. Just remember that in these hot spots lots of the food source will be rising from the bottom, suspended in mid-water or making its way to the surface to fly away. Pop into your local fly-fishing shop and they will show you what trout are eating and the imitation the trout anglers use. Now I'm not saying you should start buzzer fishing for carp but a bait fished in these areas off the bottom will give you more chance of a take than hard on the bottom. The main reason you are not getting a take on baits fished hard on the bottom is usually that the fish are in the hot spot but not on the dinner table; understand this, and your catch rate will go up: mine did.

TACKLE

It's easy to become a 'tackle tart' in carp fishing and I think that's great for you. Earn your money and you can spend it on what you want. For some reason anglers my age often have a problem with young anglers starting carp fishing, going out and buying all the kit in one go and then catching a 20lb carp. These older anglers think you should do an apprenticeship on the canal catching gudgeon first, then a roach and then making your way up, as it were, to bigger fish. That's how it worked years ago and it was certainly that way for me, but if I was a kid nowadays and I had the option of fishing for gudgeon on the canal or being surrounded by rods, rod pods and buzzers catching double-figure carp to well over 20lb all day, I'm sure the gudgeon would lose out!

Rods

I think the big problem with tackle is that a lot of articles are written by anglers fishing large gravel pits and fishing long distance with 3½lb test curve (TC) rods and big pit reels, whereas most of the readers are fishing much smaller lakes or even ponds, yet still fish with the large gravel-pit gear they have read about. This is a great shame because they are missing out on a lot of pleasure from small to medium-size carp, say 8lb to 20lb. A carp is not a great fighter – believe me, I have hooked the great fighters of the world and carp do not figure in the stakes, so you don't need heavy gear to land them.

Years ago a 1½lb TC was a standard carp rod and a 1¾lb TC was a stepped-up carp rod; now a 2½lb TC is the normal and 3½lb TC is a stepped-up job. This is way over the top in most situations and causes the angler more problems than it solves. On such powerful rods you never learn to play a carp correctly, in fact some of the most successful catchers of carp haven't got a clue how to play a fish properly!

To use the rod properly the rod should be bending to its test curve, absorbing the plunges of the fish. On a very powerful rod the angler starts back winding as soon as he feels the slightest pressure on his arm, which is how you end up with carp fights lasting half an hour to an hour. On a 2lb TC rod and 10lb line a 20lb carp shouldn't take more than five minutes to land, and a 30lb one not much more – and that's not bullying the fish, it's simply playing the fish on balanced tackle. I personally use 2¼lb TC rods in the UK, and that's fishing and landing fish to 40lb. Abroad I only use 2¾lb TC and I've landed fish to 52lb from Rainbow Lake, the snaggiest water in the world, which is like fishing in the middle of Sherwood Forest! Yet the 2¾lb TC rods handled the fish with ease and I'm confident that should I ever hook the 80lb+ record carp in there I would handle it perfectly well on my 2¾lb TC rod.

Don't get me wrong, if you have to cast great distances then you will have to step

A through-actioned 2¼lb rod with me playing a good carp. Note that I have plenty of rod rings and plenty of action in the rod.

the rod test curve up but very few anglers (including me) can make the most of carp rods over 3lb; indeed, many anglers will cast a 2¾lb TC rod further than a 3½lb TC one. Some monster casters can wind up a 3¾lb rod and get distances in excess of 150 yards but you can count the anglers

that can do this on one hand; the rest are using rods they can't use to their full potential and in reality lose out on the fight of the carp.

Now to the action of the blank. I personally go for a through-action rod because it's easier to play the carp on but all the

A margin-caught 30lb+ carp, proving that you don't need to cast 150 yards all the time.

experts will tell you a tip action rod with a powerful butt and fast tip will cast you further. The facts are that the best surf distance casters use through-action rods. Now, they don't play fish, they just cast in a field, but they still use through-action rods and they are casting over 250 yards, not 100 yards, that's good enough for me. There's the added advantage that you can play a fish much better, without line breakages or hook pulls, with a through-action rod rather than a poker stick.

The same goes for your ring spacing. An expert has written that the fewer rings you have the further the distance you will cast. Again, if you are a casting expert that may help, but for most of you a ring spacing that follows the curve of the rod will be a lot more of a pleasure when playing a fish. I class myself as an average caster. I've never been a big caster – I would like to be for some waters but never quite made the grade. I was a consultant for a number of years for North Western Blanks and designed a number of rods. One day I had the finished model of a long-range rod I had been working on delivered to me. I taped on a set of Fuji rings with the long-range setting of five to seven rings on a 12ft rod and cast with it. I then put rings on the old-fashioned way, following the curve of the rod, and guess what – it went just as far! I then put on a set of old chrome rings as opposed to the latest silicon rings, and, yes, you guessed right, still no difference! OK, I know chrome rings don't last like modern rings but after all my tests I came to the conclusion that rings needn't be as big or as few as some anglers tell you. I would go for modern rings but not so big; three-legged ones because single legs bend or break too easily for a rough bugger like me; and a sufficient number that the line follows the curve of the rod.

Reels

Looking at reels, the average angler is using reels much too big, with many using sea reels to fish park pools. The reel holds 500 yards of 10lb line and the lake he fishes is only forty yards across. With the reel most anglers use nowadays, the carp could run back to their home and still not run out of line. Surely this is crazy. I can only presume they have read that you have to have enough line on the reel to cast 150 yards and let the fish go 200 yards on its first run. I'm afraid that it simply does not happen, so choose a reel to match the rod and the venue you are fishing. Some may think it big to sit on a water with fishing tackle that's the equivalent of taking a rocket launcher to kill a rabbit. Please remember the magic words 'balanced tackle'; with my gear you will enjoy the fight of a carp and be in complete control.

Another misconception concerns the use of the clutch. A lot of carp anglers seem to think the proper way to play a carp is to 'back wind', but why is that? I ask this because, having travelled the world and fought monsters on fixed spool reels, the true experts always use the clutch. In fact, for the likes of tarpon to back wind would see you in hospital with a handful of broken knuckles. I must admit I have stood back in amazement watching some carpers playing big carp back winding every time the rod bends over literally a couple of

inches; I'm afraid with me a carp has to fight for every inch off my reel, and that way I land more and quicker. You must learn to play a fish on the clutch. Back winding is not an option, for it will eventually lose you a fish – probably the biggest you have ever hooked.

Line

There are a thousand brands of line but I only use a couple for my carp fishing. In snag-free waters I use 16lb or 20lb Diawa Infinity, which is memory-free, smooth and a lovely casting line, although its anti-abrasion quality is not up to the standard of some other lines. My main line for years was Gold Label 'Pro Gold', which never let me down, but the last couple of years I have used Kryston 'Kryptonite' on the recommendation of a mate of mine who said he had caught a number of big fish with it that had run him into snags. I can confirm it's tremendous line. I use the 12lb in England and the 18lb abroad, and great stuff it is.

I know lots of anglers are moving on to braid, but for me it's the last resort for I hate braid! I don't like what it does to the fish when it wraps around them and I detest the 'feel' of braid when playing a fish, which is the most important thing for me as I must enjoy the fight. I have used braid in the past and I will use it in the future when great distances are required on huge French reservoirs but it's definitely a last resort.

These are the most important items of tackle. The rest, like buzzers, indicators, bait boats, clothes, water containers, hold-alls and carryalls and so on, won't lose or catch you fish like a rod, reel and line. All I will say is, don't fall for the cheapest but go for the best you can afford. Cheap copies are fine if you fish twice a year, but if you fish once, twice or more a week then go for the best as it will be worth it in the long run. My parting note on tackle is, have a decent rod, reel and line but make sure you buy the very, very best for the rigs and bait. Let's face it: that's what the fish see and pick up – they don't have a clue how you look on the bank!

BAIT

I could write a book on baits but in fact I am only going to write about the ones I use regularly and that I have caught carp on. Too many 'bait gurus' sit in the kitchen dreaming up ideas and never catching fish or even go fishing. I'm an angler who knows about baits that catch me a lot of carp and I keep it simple, which I'm sure will please you. I will put my favourite baits into various categories to make it even more simple.

Boilies

Up to about eight years ago a boilie to me was a ready-made bait from a good company like Richworth that caught me a lot of fish. I used the likes of Tutti Frutti wherever I went and my indicators usually went off a few times a session. Then I joined a syndicate water with big fish and top carpers, and to cut a long story short I simply couldn't get a take. Now don't get me wrong, I haven't fished it for hundreds of hours without any takes at all but I blanked a couple of times while watching other anglers catch. I didn't like that! One of those catching was Brian Gardner, a well-known carper who had done the circuit waters for a number of years. I'm not proud and asked his advice; he said, 'you need a top-quality bait – one that the fish eat loads of as a food source and that will last all season'. I took his advice, although I didn't think carp were that clever. How

wrong can you be? Brian knocked me up a Red Premier fishmeal boilie with SBS Frankfurter Sausage flavour at a low level and the first time out I'm into a 38lb mirror: a personal best at the time. It was from this point I started to look at my baits a little more closely rather than just buying a ready-made boilie that everyone was using.

It's common knowledge now that four years ago I bought SBS Baits, a well-known bait company for thirty years and indeed one of the first bait companies in the UK. I needed a bait to use as a flagship for the company, so together with Tony Mills and Wayne Dunn set out to design a bait that could catch anywhere quickly and be a long-lasting bait. Guess what we ended up with? A red fishmeal boilie and yes, you've guessed it, SBS Frankfurter Sausage at low levels. We called it the M1 and it caught on everywhere. This bait is still my main line attack on most waters I fish, although I do change a couple of the attractors and take out the Robin Red – which gives it the colour – on that fish have been hammered on it in its normal state. Using the basic mix and messing around with different attractors and flavours, I will use this bait probably till I die, that's how much the carp love this bait. That 38-pounder I caught years ago was caught on basically the same bait as I have used recently to catch a 51lb and a 52lb carp. A good bait is a good bait forever.

Some anglers will tell you fishmeal boilies are near to useless in the winter, but I'm afraid that's an old wives' tale – neither I nor my field testers have ever found this to be so. Having said that, in the winter I do like to 'open' the boilie up more by adding the likes of ground rape seed and finely ground oyster shell, which helps to release the attractants. On this subject, I think it's fair to say that a lot of carp anglers in Britain want their boilie to last a couple of days in the water. Now that's fine

The 38lb+ fish that changed my thinking on boilies.

with your hookbait, but with your freebies you want them to break down so they release the attractants and flavour into the water; these are no good locked into a boilie for days. I will let you into a big secret of mine: to all the baits I use I add a teaspoonful of SBS 'The Edge' to the 1kg dry mix. This Corn Steep Liquor-based powder leaks into the water out of the boilie straight away and carp love it! In some mixes 'The Edge' will start to leak out even before it enters the water and form a light-coloured dusting on the outside of the

boilie. You could mistake this for mould setting in, but it most definitely is not.

I do use a couple of other boilies. One is a two-coloured boilie, which is half yellow – a rich creamy seed mix flavoured with Old English Toffee – and half a red fish-meal mix with no added flavour but with extra Black Pepper Essential Oil. Carp love the sweet and sour taste and the two colours break the shape up when it's sitting on the bottom, making it different from what most anglers are using. My other boilie is a great favourite of mine in winter

163

(when I may only put out a single bait or a three-boilie stringer and expect one take all day if I'm lucky) and that's good old Richworth Tutti Frutti in freezer form, not ready-made. I like the freezer Tutti because they go sticky after a day or two out of the freezer and I think they become more attractive to the carp then. I would not bait up with these boilies, for I don't think the fish eat a lot of them, but they cannot resist picking up one or two, which is all you need on a cold winter's day.

There are hundreds of boilies for sale and some great companies making bait. The only thing I would suggest to you is to keep away from cheap bait that is such a stodgy texture that it doesn't break down for days or even weeks. These are bad for fishing and more importantly bad for the fish. Quality bait is a must: I learnt that years ago. So people who use cheap ingredients are kidding themselves. They cannot compete with quality ingredients.

Shape and Size

Let's move on to a very important aspect of baits and that's shape and size. Ninety-nine times out of a hundred nowadays I use pellet-shaped boilies only because most other anglers use round-shaped boilies. The day anglers start using pellet-shaped ones, I will start using round ones.

Size is even more important, and to be different from the norm – which is 16mm – you can drop down a size to, say, a 12mm boilie or go up a couple of sizes to a 22mm, both of which will score on heavily fished waters. I nowadays rarely use big boilies, usually fishing with 12mm ones in England and 14mm abroad. If I want to step up the size of bait I will put two or even three smaller baits on. The nice thing about this set-up is that you can throw in a pop-up with the sinkers and start achieving a 'neutral density' set-up (which I will talk about in the rig section). I know some anglers say

they never use pop-ups or a snowman set-up because they are unnatural but to be honest, any boilie, wherever it is sitting, is unnatural. In fact, at times the more unnatural it is, the more carp it will catch. For example, a small boilie fished zig-rig style four feet off the bottom is as unnatural as you can get, but boy, does this rig catch. So remember, don't fish all your boilies hard on the bottom – experiment. The most frustrating thing is that most anglers only give such rigs a try on a day when all their favourite methods are failing. The chances are that you're not catching because the carp are not feeding so actually nothing will work, when you try a new method and it fails you rarely give it a go again. This is unfair on the method. The time to experiment on one rod is the day the fish are moving and you are having runs on other methods. That's the only way that you will gain confidence with a new approach, thus adding another method to your armoury.

Particles

I'm not a great lover of many particles. I always think anglers who use lots of them are too tight to buy boilies, plus for me they always attract the smaller fish! Having said that, I do use a couple of particles. I use hemp seed that has been soaked in Corn Steep Liquor, especially if I'm pre-baiting a water. But even then I will break up the boilies I am going to use and put these into the hemp. I don't use hemp as a hookbait; I will still fish a boilie over the top of the bed of hemp. Some anglers will say the biggest hemp seed is the best; well, I would agree if you're fishing it on the hook for roach, but as far as baiting up for carp is concerned it doesn't matter how small or big it is.

I will use soaked maize or sweetcorn on 'new' waters that have rarely been fished;

The Method with plastic corn.

indeed that bait would be my first choice even before boilies, but – and it's a big but – I rarely use maize or sweetcorn in Britain to bait up with, for I think on a lot of English waters sweetcorn is looked upon as a danger signal. But as with the Tutti Frutti boilie, I will very often have one rod on two pieces of plastic corn (the best, in my opinion, is from Enterprise Tackle). I put on one piece of sinker and one piece of pop-up corn; this will see the hook on the bed of the lake and the two pieces of plastic corn popped up snowman style. Like with the Tutti Frutti boilie, carp will be inquisitive and pick it up … too late! Some anglers think that plastic corn is only good in clear water as a visible bait but from my experience I disagree, I think the carp actually like the smell of the plastic! I will confidently use it in coloured water and at night, taking many carp in such situations.

I've never been a great user of tiger nuts, but they are great for waters with lots of nuisance fish and crayfish, which eat boilies in minutes. In such a situation I will use a tiger nut but I am never as confident as when I have a boilie on the end. I'm never sure carp eat a lot of tiger nuts, so when I fish these I pop them up snowmen style, so with a bit of luck it's the first one to go in the carp's mouth before it clears off.

Pellets

I have put pellets under the banner of particles, but I do use lots of pellets. My favourite pellet is a mix of all sorts, which I call my 'Multi Mix'. This includes high-oil trout pellets, low-oil carp pellets, hemp pellets, Corn Steep Liquor pellets, maize pellets, squid pellets and lobworm pellets, all in different sizes and shapes. I just think this confuses the carp and keeps them occupied in the swim longer. I'm sure they are like dogs, sorting out their favourite morsels from the bowl before eating the lot; get a carp doing this in your swim and he's as good as in the landing net.

If I were to use one pellet, it would be Corn Steep Liquor pellets because they

CSL pellets are always worth putting into a swim to keep fish coming back time and time again.

dissolve completely in ten minutes, leaving a pulp on the bed of the lake. The carp eat this but cannot eat it all, as a lot of it rises in the water as they feed. After the carp have left the area, the small particles settle down again, ensuring that there is always an attractor in the swim. With pellets that last for ages, a carp comes in and eats them all, leaving nothing for the next carp. Using Corn Steep Liquor pellets solves the age-old problem of whether there is anything left in the swims to attract fish: you know there is always a residue left in the swim.

Groundbait

This is an area that for years big carp anglers left alone, classing it as a match man's method, but modern-day carp anglers have realized that the use of ground-baits can be a great way of attracting and keeping carp in a swim. Certainly on the continent on the huge waters, such as St Cassien, using groundbait has accounted for many fish. A method that has made the groundbait easy to apply is actually called 'the Method' and involves moulding the groundbait around a specially designed feeder and casting the whole lot into the swim. This has proved devastating on some waters, but to be fair soon 'blows': the loud noise of it hitting the water initially attracts the fish to the area but once a few fish have been caught the loud noise becomes a repellent rather than an attractant and then the method stops catching.

Groundbait does not stop catching even after the Method has blown, especially if you have the use of a boat or bait boats. With these aids you can put the groundbait in very accurately and quietly, which is a must if you have to fish short sessions. The long-stay angler can make all the noise he wants for he has a day or even two for the swim to recover, but if you scare the fish in the area and you are only fishing a twelve-hour session you may very well blank!

There are many good groundbaits on the market, but regardless which is your favourite, I would recommend you add Corn Steep Liquor meal and 'The Edge'. What will happen with the Corn Steep Liquor meal is, as I explained above with the Corn Steep Liquor pellets, that is, there will always be a residue in the swim. 'The Edge' I simply put in everything, I'm that confident it will keep carp in the area. I would add 250g of Corn Steep Liquor meal and a teaspoon of 'The Edge' to a kilo of dry groundbait. I would then take out some lake water, add a cap of Corn Steep Liquor liquid and mix it up.

There is a knack to mixing groundbait that match anglers have, but few carp anglers ever master. For a start you need a shallow round bowl, not a deep square tub where dry mix can get trapped in the corners, making a very uneven mix. Do a small amount at a time and then only 'dampen' the mix thoroughly at first and leave for fifteen to thirty minutes; that way the bigger particles, like flake maize, will have a chance to absorb the water rather than still being dry and floating on the top once the ball breaks up. Then mix to the texture you require.

That texture will depend on how you are going to get the bait out. If I'm using a catapult I mix the balls up hard, basically using the same mix as for the Method; if I'm using a bait boat I will put more boilie bits in there which wouldn't hold together on a catapult. In a boat sometimes, especially in shallow water, I will introduce the mix as a 'slop' – I am literally able to pour the stuff in. This puts a cloud in the water, which carp love and will come great distances to investigate.

Another tip: I also like my groundbaits dark. I'm not into white groundbait, in fact one of my favourite groundbaits has Robin Red added, which obviously turns the bait red. Unnatural as it may sound, the carp love it although it would not be so successful if you just added a dye or red groundbait, for the Robin Red itself is a great attractor.

If you want to get carp on to a boilie mix and flavour cheaply and quickly, try putting some of the base mix and flavour into your groundbait and pre-bait with this. I remember when we developed the M1 at the Monument that although we introduced lots of boilies, the bulk of attractions was M1-flavoured groundbait and pellets – so for anyone using an M1, the fish recognize the flavour as a food source.

'The Edge': I swear by it in any carp bait.

Other Baits

There are many other baits for carp. In fact, other than chub, I think the carp has the most varied diet of any fish swimming. The likes of luncheon meat, sweetcorn and paste are self-explanatory, although I do wish beginners especially would realize the value of paste (the base mix) wrapped around the boilie before you cast out. This breaks down in an hour or so and leaves a lovely attractant around the bait and rig. Another bait worth mentioning here is cockles, a super change bait when the carp are off the boilies for a short time.

A tiger nut tipped with plastic corn of floating type: a good bait where crayfish are present.

Every season carp will turn off the boilie and will become almost impossible to catch, especially if it's a naturally rich water. This happened in the summer of 2005 at the famous Monument Fishery, run by good friend Rob Hales. Everyone, and I mean everyone, was struggling and Rob was rather worried because fifteen anglers blanking every day is not good for business. Rob asked me what I thought, and I said there's only one thing for it, and that's feeder maggots.

Lots of big carp anglers will class maggots as a match bait, but they are a great big carp bait too, especially in waters like the Monument, where there are no other species than carp. On my first session there I did a feature with *Angling Times* carp editor Steve Broad, where he fished boilies and blanked. Steve is a very good carp angler and this just illustrates how the

A 37lb mirror: part of a brace of 30lb+ fish caught on maggots.

Maggots are a great bait, even for monster carp.

fishing had gone. I fished a large Drennan Feeder with hair-rigged maggots and caught eight carp and lost one right next to Steve. Included in the catch was the lake record common and a 32lb mirror, that's how good maggots can be. In fact, over the next month, I caught twenty-five fish, including many twenties and half a dozen thirties. One evening I landed a 37lb+ mirror, and whilst taking the photos, a 39lb+ mirror picked up the other feeder maggot rig! On venues where you would otherwise expect a fish a session, you can empty the place on maggots.

RIGS AND BAITING

There is more nonsense talked about rigs than any other branch of carp fishing. Don't get me wrong, modern rigs are brilliant and on most water you have to think a little about your rigs to get the edge over the other anglers on the water.

Now I could easily write a chapter full of diagrams of rigs involving all sorts of bits of silicon tube, shrink tube, blobs of lead and so on, but you have probably seen all those before.

What I have to contribute to a rig section is 'be different'. It's easy enough to see or hear what other anglers are using, and if you use exactly the same then common sense will tell you that the best catches you can achieve are the same as theirs. That's OK if they are emptying the place but more often than not what happens is something like this: most anglers on the water catch very little, then one person starts catching a lot more than everyone else, maybe because of a bait but also because of his rig, then everyone copies him and everyone catches till the fish wise up and it's back to few captures until someone else thinks of something different.

Now you can be one of the followers or the leader, which is actually easier than most people think. Let me give you a few

With mussels like this you need a mainline that you can trust.

examples. First off, if you can, always back lead; obviously in weedy waters and snaggy waters you cannot, but when you can, make it a priority, for lines in the water can be the biggest turn-off for all fish, especially big, old, wise carp. Now make sure the last six feet of your rig is sitting hard, and I mean hard, on the bottom. I use at the moment either TFG or ESP lead-core braided leaders, which sink like a rock and take on the contours of the lake, which is a must.

I am going to assume you know how to put a bait on a hair-rig, whether it be a pop-up or sinking bait. A couple of important tips here. The hooklength material you must get right. I have come full circle with this and I'm back using 12lb clear monofilament line with a 2lb piece of monofilament on the hair. I don't like to use a knotless knot on heavy mono as it simply does not react right for me when the carp pick up the bait. I use a blow-back rig with the hair held in place with a small piece of silicone tube down the shank of the hook. This system works best with materials that allow the bait to move back up the shank, and this is impossible with heavy monofilament. I am using mono because most anglers don't, it's as simple as that.

My favourite braid is Super Nova and my least favourite – although I do use it on single baits fished at a distance to help stop tangling – are the plastic-covered braids

I like barbed hooks because carp don't drop out.

like snake skin. I do occasionally use them, but it's difficult for an all-rounder like me who is used to fishing for roach on 1½lb line hooklengths, to then suddenly expect a carp to pick up a hooklength that looks like it came out of an electrician's toolbox. It works, I just don't like it!

Nowadays, following my mate Rob Hales' success, I always use a marker pen to black out my hooklength and prefer black hooks and black swivels – in fact have everything black because most lakes and ponds are black on the bottom rather than silver. I use hooklengths six to eight inches long; I know some anglers use four-inch hooklengths but I never go that short but I have found in the past that big fish, especially, fall off.

Hooks cause some anglers loads of problems mainly because they keep changing patterns, sometimes trying every pattern that hits the market with some famous angler's name on. Let's get one thing straight: just because an angler catches a 50lb carp doesn't mean he knows how to develop and design a good hook. One

171

minute the guy's a pipe-fitter, the next he is a hook designer, well I don't think so! Peter Drennan knows about hooks and that's what I use. For years I used Super Specialists and now I use his boilie hooks or his ESP Raptors, and I step up to Extra Strong Gamakatsu when fishing snaggy swims abroad for 60lb fish. If I never use any other hooks for the next fifty years it wouldn't bother me. I have very few fish fall off, the hooks don't bend or break and I'm completely confident in the hook. Some anglers never achieve this state, which is crazy, and even if they do some still feel impelled to change.

Whatever hooks I use in most situations I will try to counteract the weight of the hook, even on baits that are hard on the bottom. This can be achieved by making your own 'neutral density' hookbaits, which in layman's terms means the bait sinks to the bottom very, very slowly. With a boilie I achieve this by adding cork dust to the base mix or a small piece of floating plastic sweetcorn to the boilie on the hair. The goal is to make the actual hookbait react the same as the freebies when the carp comes over the bait and feeds.

This is an appropriate point to bring up the debate on barbed versus unbarbed hooks. Anglers using unbarbed hooks like them because if you get one caught in your jumper or net it comes out more easily, and it's much simpler to unhook a fish and supposedly does the fish a lot less damage. I do believe this on match fisheries, where match anglers are playing small fish on poles and hooking the same fish day in and day out, and I don't fish such waters probably never will; I want to fish a water where I may only hook a particular fish once in my lifetime, and when I do I want a great, big, barbed hook in it that won't fall out so when I land it I have to use forceps to get the hook out! I firmly believe that a barbed hook moves less in a carp's mouth than an unbarbed version and so actually does less damage, especially in a long fight with a big fish.

BAITING UP

Baiting up is probably one of the most important aspects of fishing and something that I am good at, if I say so myself. I have put this subject away from the bait section because it is a completely different subject and very few anglers get it right. Baiting up takes understanding of the situation on the day or through the session, and sometimes that only comes with experience. Having said that, hopefully I can help you with the basics.

The fundamental mistake a lot of carp anglers make in baiting up is to fill the swim in at the start of the session with a spod packed with 5kg of particles and 2kg of boilies, then sit back and wait for the fish to come along. In a lot of cases this method does catch a lot of big fish despite being wrong! If you have three or four days to sit on a water, you can do almost everything wrong but still catch fish and indeed if you catch a couple of monsters, you may even be deemed an expert, when in reality you are a poor angler who spends a lot of time on the bank.

Very often the swim, having been bombarded with all that bait, can then be dead for twelve to twenty-four hours, which is not much good if your session is only that long (which it probably is if you work and have kids and a wife). In this situation it's better to quickly put out a couple of PVA bags on the rig full of a 'bag mix', which for me would always include Corn Steep Liquor products for the reasons mentioned above under Groundbait. Then I would introduce twenty or thirty boilies, probably 14mm, but larger if you need to get them out further.

Waiting for a take at dusk, a great time for carp.

I tend to make up my freebies to a consistency that can be catapulted out but then breaks up within a few hours. Obviously I make my hookbait a little different, so they will last up to 24 hours. But those freebies I want to break up quickly to let all the attractants into the water to do their job and attract the carp. When they break down they will be eaten by all the other species present, so I know that I won't end up just piling bait on top of bait if I have not had a take. Otherwise, if you put out thirty boilies and after a few hours there are no takes, you don't know whether this is because the carp have eaten the freebies and not eaten the hookbaits, or because they have not even been in the swim, in which case the bait is still lying there. My way, I just keep topping up, knowing the activity of the boilies going in the swim will attract carp, and more importantly I've not put more bait on the top of the initial bait I put in.

If you do get a take after a couple of hours the chances are all the boilies there have been eaten, because I always work on

173

the principle that my hookbait is the last one to be taken. So now I put another twenty to thirty boilies in the area and start over. If the same thing happens again you are having a red letter day, just keep reeling them in and repeat, putting the same number of boilies out each time. This only happens on rare occasions; generally you have to top up the peg and wait a lot longer for a take.

On waters where there are a lot of fish, and big fish at that, like some of the waters in France, I would start the session off with a 20kg bag of Corn Steep Liquor pellets spread around the area. This will normally keep fish around the area for days. After four days, I would put another 20kg bag in there, especially if I caught a lot of fish in the first four days and I know there are still a lot about. This may seem a lot

of bait but when 30–50lb carp are about, half a dozen fish can see that lot away – believe me, they don't grow that big eating little!

You will hear anglers say that you have to be accurate with your baiting – 'on a sixpence' is a common saying – but I will scatter my bait everywhere over a large area, as I find getting the carp moving around searching for food gives me more takes. Having three rods, three lines, loads of bait and loads of fish in an area as big as a sixpence will make the job more difficult. I always try to imagine what is going on in my swim. With bait spread over a large area, the carp are basically chasing around for another morsel of food; when a morsel is spotted by two or even more fish then the chase is on to see who takes it in their mouth first. This is better than two, three

A big 30lb mirror from the Monument Fishery.

or more fish tails up in a confined area all eating away without affecting one another. If the fish are feeding over a larger area you have more chance of hooking and landing a fish without scaring the rest, which is common sense when you think about it.

Sometimes I take completely the opposite tack and introduce no freebies, just a stringer over a twenty-four-hour session. This is rare for me but I will do it, even though I couldn't tell you what would make me resort to this; sometimes my instincts just tell me that not many fish are feeding and so a lot of bait in a spot would be counter-productive. Sometimes a couple of hours before going home I will fire a load of boilies into the peg even if I have caught nothing, in the hope that the influx of a lot of bait will get the fish head down. Very often when the fishing is hard, I will use feeder maggots as suggested earlier under Other Baits, and will start off by putting six to ten casts in the swim without a hooklength to get some maggots in the swim, then tie a hooklength on and cast every thirty minutes. Rarely does this method blank. If possible I will be doing this in an area a good distance from my other rods. If I'm fishing a water like the Monument where there are no other species, I will fish both rods on the maggot and be working them all day every thirty minutes. This is a deadly method at this venue and anywhere, for that matter.

Whatever the bait, rig or method, getting your baiting-up programme right is the difference between one fish a trip or a dozen. As I write this, my mate Rob Hales is in St Cassien on the south coast of France and, using the same strategy as mine, with quick dissolving boilies as freebies and has taken ten carp in ten hours. Most anglers don't get that in a season from this difficult water.

ENJOYMENT AND HUNTER INSTINCTS

Let's get one thing straight: the whole reason that I go carp fishing is for enjoyment. I rarely let it stress me out. After a bad session I don't feel like kicking the cat up in the air, and I thank the sport for all the enjoyment it has given me. Unfortunately, in carp fishing something happens in the carp angler's head that makes lots of people leave the sport after a few years really dejected and even feeling let down. I don't think this happens so much to Mr Average because he has it right – he simply goes carp fishing for pleasure and to get away from the hassles of everyday life. Catching a big carp is a bonus and he will certainly take photos, but he has no designs to be famous, write articles and see his face splashed everywhere.

Perhaps surprisingly, however, there are a lot of anglers who, having caught a few carp, do want to be famous, have their photos in the press and indeed earn their living from the sport. Many of you will say, 'it must be great earning your living from being a carp angler'. It is, but to make it in this sport is not easy and for every one like me who earns his living from the sport, many more fail and sadly fall out with the sport forever. If there is one thing I can say here to help anyone to make a living out of going fishing, then it's simply go out and catch fish and enjoy it in the first instance.

Remember the sport owes you nothing. Some anglers argue that they've put a lot into it and that now it's their turn to take something out. I say that from the moment I caught my first fish I started taking a great deal from this sport, so it owes me nothing. I made it in this sport by going fishing, catching good fish and writing about it. Had I not become well known and been asked to contribute to books like

What a fish!

this one, I would have still been fishing like I am now: the only difference would have been that very few people would have known my name.

Having said that about enjoyment, I am still a hunter and take my fishing very seriously. It always astounds me how many carp anglers have not got the basic hunter instinct, which in the long run will catch a lot more fish. How many of you, when you have selected your swim, pile all your gear in it. Then you set up the bivvy, which involves knocking at least eight tent pegs in the ground. Then you set up your bed-chair, guest chair, cooking equipment and of course put your rod rests in or set up your pod. Now let me ask you a question: having selected the peg because you think

there are fish there, why have you done your best to scare the lot away?

Try this approach instead. Most of you will have your rods made up, so having selected your swim simply cast at least one rod out a nd wait for an hour or two before starting and more importantly, quietly put your equipment in your peg. I have to say that unless it's cold or going to rain, I don't set a bivvy up till just on dark because I think fish can see them, and they know anglers are about when there are bivvies all around the lake. I'm positive that if all anglers came to an agreement not to use bivvies until dark more fish would be caught. I would go a step further, and say that on heavily fished waters sometimes when the carp roll they are looking for danger on land. Some of you will think I'm mad saying that, but I firmly believe that fish roll at times not for feeding but to look around the lake!

Because carp anglers fish long sessions they can become sloppy in their hunting instincts and become loud on the bank. They wash their plates up, their mates stand in the swim talking for hours on end, they laugh loudly, even shouting to their mates over on the other side of the lake. All this will stop you catching carp. Taking this further, there are ways of casting leads, spods and marker floats that make minimum noise. Learn to 'feather' casts down, as this will save you a lot of disturbances. The same goes for returning your rig. Why is it that when 99 per cent of carp anglers return their rig it usually involves a 3oz lead attached across the surface of the lake splashing all the way back to the swim. There is no need for this – if you hold the rod down low and reel you can bring the lead back to the bank with no sound or splash.

Don't rest your landing net against the skyline so fish can see it; put it down ready for landing a fish. Wear fishing clothes in green or brown. Of course you can keep a bright red shirt for photos but when you are fishing dress like a hunter, not a speedway rider. I personally don't go for all the latest camouflage gear. I don't like to look like everyone else on the bank, plus I could afford a trip abroad carp fishing for the cost of the stuff, but, joking apart, at least it's better than gear designed for nightclubs and pop festivals. I must admit I do like those big sheets of camouflaged netting you can buy and put up as a screen in the swim, leaving only a gap for the rods and playing the fish; these will help catch a lot of fish. I know some of you will think I'm taking this a little too far, but would you act the same if you were twenty yards away from a rabbit you were hoping to shoot? Of course you wouldn't, so why be different with a carp if you don't want to scare it away?

Let me tell you something I learned when I first went trout fishing on a big lake. My friend and expert trout angler said I should sit down after a few hours and have a cup of coffee and sandwich, even have a sleep for an hour, and let everyone else scare all the fish into my swim with their casting. It worked then and it does now, not only for trout. Having spodded out or baited up on a crowded lake at the start of the day, don't cast in for an hour. I know that's hard to do when you only have one day fishing a week but it will be worth it, believe me. Let all the other anglers miscast and cast again. Most anglers will have two or three attempts before they put the rods on the rest and that's with every rod, which adds up to a lot of casting if there's fifteen other anglers on the bank and all through this your swim hasn't had a line or lead in it. Fish will move into your peg, start feeding confidently and by the time you've scared them like everyone else you would have had a carp or two. I will pull my rods in every day for a couple of hours and have a sleep or a walk around the lake. You will be surprised how many times my mates have said 'you lucky bugger' when I have then caught straight away on my return. That's not luck; again, it's just common sense. You are a hunter, so act like one.

MEMORABLE FISH

I really could write a whole book on memorable carp I have caught, some from canals, farm ponds, lakes and even inland seas, but what I'm going to tell you about is my first double-figure fish, my first 20lb+, then my first 30lb+, then my first 40lb+, then my first 50lb+ (in the future my name

A 47lb common: the best-looking carp I have caught in my whole life.

is on a 60lb+ but that's something to look forward to, and I just hope it's English and the British record!).

First Double

My first double came from a small pond near Halesowen in the Black Country. I had my dad's demob coat and my grandad's floppy hat, for I wanted to look like my hero, Dick Walker. I had an Edgar Sealey fibreglass carp rod, an Intrepid Elite reel and potatoes as bait. I was a budding specimen hunter, and though I caught very little, I enjoyed just looking and acting the same as my *Angling Times* hero. Little did I know that twenty years later I would be writing a column in the same paper. Dick is dead now but I still fish a lot according to his written word.

Anyway, contrary to what Dick said about potatoes, they were a useless bait for me and once I realized that, I started to catch carp. I caught them on maggots, bread and lobworm just like any other fish.

This particular day I was fishing a piece of bread flake on a ledger, the line draped over my Heron bite alarm and as usual blanking, when I saw a 'massive' carp of about ten pounds swimming in front of me. I flicked a piece of crust to it, knowing full well it wouldn't take it but instead speed away. To my amazement, it opened its big mouth and swallowed the lot. I couldn't believe it so I did it again, and, guess what, it did the same again!

Now, even a young novice like me didn't need telling twice that I had actually found a carp without a brain. I quickly bit off the rig and replaced it with just a size 2 Sundridge carp hook (I think the number of the hook was 9284, a great hook at the time). I put a big piece of crust on and cast in right on the carp's head. Had the fish been a normal carp, he would have run for his life, but not this one: he pushed the crust upwards with his nose, opened his mouth and again swallowed the lot. I can still remember like it was yesterday, though it's forty years ago now, looking in amazement and not striking, and only knowing a fish was on when the rod was nearly pulled out my hands. I landed the fish in my Efgeco net and weighed it in an onion sack. It weighed 11lb I was on my way.

Twenty-Pounder

Twenty pounds was the next stop. But there was a problem getting my twenty-pounder for there were very few lakes in the Midlands that held such fish. I did come close a couple of times, in fact my 19½lb common from Kyre Pool near Tenbury Wells was a personal best for years but no twenty-pound carp. Then I met a young man by the name of Dave Sparks. He was a carp expert – so much so, he had two carp rods and Mitchell reels and even knew famous carp anglers who had fished Redmire Pool. My eyes opened like saucers and my jaw dropped as he told me stories of 20lb, even 25lb+ fish on a lake in the middle of Llandindrod Wells in Wales. I couldn't get up there quick enough in my Allegro estate, my wife even lent me money out of the kitty for the kids' school clothes to buy the petrol. I did it for a season and caught carp up to 18lb, including three doubles in a day like Tag Barnes, another hero of mine.

But the next summer was to open with a bang. I could not make the morning of the 16th, 'opening day' in the old days, but arrived with Dave Sparks on the evening and fished that night. As usual in carp fishing in those days we caught nothing through the night until 10.30am, when my rod had a 'special' paste on the hook (cat meat and trout pellet powder, in fact). This rod had a coil of silver paper as the indicator and this coil nearly went through the rings as the take from a big fish took place. I bent into the fish, looked at Dave and said, 'this is it'. He knew what I meant and got the landing net ready. Great carp

anglers like John Lilley, Chris Yates and Ron Felton had all taken their first twenty-pound carp here and I was hoping this was mine. After a fight that took ages I finally landed the beast and with shaking hands weighed a 20lb 14oz mirror carp – what a fish. I got drunk that night and never fished, I was so over the moon. Later that year Dave Sparks caught his first 20lb+ carp. After that we never went back, as the job had been done.

Thirty-Pounder

Between my first twenty-pounder and my first thirty-pounder a good number of years passed, for I enjoyed fishing for anything with fins on, which took me all around the world, so English carp were not really on my mind. But then Rob Hales acquired a small lake we nicknamed 'Woodpecker Pool' because of the number of great spotted woodpeckers that lived around the lake. This water held fish to just under 40lb – a fish known as the 'big mirror' for obvious reasons. This was a delightful water that I will describe in more detail later in the chapter under Favourite Venues. It was a small pool with only thirteen carp in total, plus a couple of 30lb+ plus cats, so it wasn't easy; some good anglers had failed there, which was no disgrace.

The place was good to me. I rarely blanked and soon had a number of fish under my belt, but 'only' twenties. Then one day, fishing off the dam, I had a take on a boilie the same as from any other carp from the water, but this one kept real deep – in fact I never saw the fish until it was in the net. I knew straightaway it was the 'big mirror' at a spawned-out weight of 32lb 8oz and I was over the moon. I caught this fish again at a later date at 38lb 8oz, it was a lucky fish for me. This carp was also a milestone in that at the time it meant that in England I had caught thirty-pound cats, thirty-pound pike and now thirty-pound carp. I think at the time only a handful of people had done this before me.

Forty-Pounder

Believe it or not, before I had a thirty-pounder in England I caught a 40lb+ leather carp in France, and what a fish that was back in 1988! It was from the mighty St Cassien, on my first visit, after I had only been in the water four hours – how lucky is that? Again I was with my old mate Rob Hales. I remember arriving at the lake driving over the hill that brings you to the South Arm. I was blown away and couldn't believe the size of the place – I thought the South Arm was the whole lake. I found out minutes later there was another two arms, the West and the North, which were just as big; as I said, I was blown away.

It was just on dark and we decided to hire a boat and row around to see if we could spot any fish. 'Spot any fish' proved to be the understatement of the year. We came near to a place known as 'Ellis Point', where Kevin Ellis had previously caught a 70lb+ fish; can you believe that, a 70lb+ in 1986? As we approached the swim in the dark someone started to throwing cows off the cliff into the water, or that's what it sounded like. I remember saying 'what the hell is that?' to which Rob said, 'carp'. I said he had to be joking. He wasn't: there were forty-, fifty- and sixty-pound fish jumping out of the water and the waves were rocking the boat, I kid you not.

To cut a long story short, we put some bait on their heads and fished there next morning. Only four hours after casting out I had a take that was a 'single noter' and straight away I knew I had beaten my 27½lb personal best of the time. We rowed out in the boat to land it. The water was so deep and so clear I made a fool of myself,

suggesting to Rob it was big tench. I swear I had never seen a carp twenty feet down in clear water, and it looked like a 7lb yellow tench. As it came further up in the water it became a twenty-pound carp, then a thirty-pound carp, then, as it neared the surface, we shook with excitement for it was twice as big as anything we had ever seen – some tench! We got it in the net and rowed back to the shore like two kids. Rob hugged me and was as pleased as me, a true mate. It weighed 40lb 8oz, and it was a leather with not a scale on its body.

Fifty-Pounder

When I caught my first double-figure fish I didn't weigh much over fifty pounds myself, and yet here I was trying to catch a carp that big!

When I had my first fifty-pounder it was just one of those days: I just knew I was going to catch it. The day from start to finish was like something out of a book, you just could not write a script better. I was supposed to be travelling down to Rainbow Lake as always with Rob Hales but my niece Michelle had decided to get married and my wife Margaret informed me if I missed it the consequences could be serious. Rob kindly drove the gear and bait down to Rainbow Lake, some eleven hours from home, whilst I got drunk at the wedding. The next day I was to fly from Birmingham to Bordeaux, then take a €90 taxi ride to the lake.

The problem was the plane had a three-and-a-half-hour delay and I was still hung over from the wedding bash. Whilst taking breakfast, a guy who played golf at my wife's golf club came up and asked me where I was going, and I told him. Can you believe that he had a holiday home thirty minutes from Rainbow Lake and as he was passing the lake he would give me a lift. I offered him the money but he would not

A 50lb+ unbelievable fish.

accept; my first bit of luck. When, true to his word, he took me to Peg 19, a rather shocked Rob couldn't believe my luck. After we had said our goodbyes, Rob straight away told me of a 'certainty' of a horse his father owned that was running in 30 minutes' time and on which he had put a few bob. Having saved the equivalent of £50 on the taxi, I thought I'd blow it on the horse. Rob phoned my bet into his bookie and we awaited the result. You've guessed it, the horse romped home and I was now £200 to the good.

I set up the rest of my gear; Rob had put up things like my bivvy while he waited for me to arrive. I remember saying, 'what a day, if only I could catch my first 50lb+ carp, what a hat trick that would be.' Three

hours later, at 5pm, I had a run in the snaggiest part of the lake at 150 yards out. We jumped in the boat and to our amazement the fish had swum around in circles instead of swimming into the snags. We rowed back to the bank and Rob weighed the fish, a massive mirror, at 52lb. Now, that's what you call a lucky day. I should have done the lottery.

FAVOURITE CARP VENUES

I have picked four of my favourite venues, two in England, one in France and one in Spain; all four mean a lot to me. You have to remember I never fish anywhere a lot because I fish for so many species and on

LEFT: A 48lb+ mirror: what a kipper!

BELOW: A big, fat Rainbow Lake 50lb+ beauty.

so many venues, but these four I fell in love with right from the start and will always remember fondly.

Acton Burnell

The first is the lower lake at Acton Burnell, one of Rob Hales' syndicate waters where 'Bill', the 50lb+ common, swims. To say the lower and indeed the upper lake are beautiful is an understatement of the carp world. While fishing you may well see a wild otter, buzzards, treecreepers and corn buntings. Hugh Miles, that famous wildlife photographer, was lucky enough to film an osprey taking a rudd from the surface whilst filming Martin Bowler catching a 44lb common on the float. I used to sit there behind the big wooden gates living the life I had only dreamed of years ago. Many people have seen the closed doors of the fishery but a very few have actually stepped through and sampled this incredible fishery. The fish are unpressured; indeed, if you spend too much time up there catching fish, Rob will have you out of the syndicate. He wants you to catch fish and enjoy the place but he doesn't like 'full-timers' staying on the lake, keeping the swims to themselves, like on so many southern circuit waters.

I remember one night fishing with Ritchie Allen. We were fishing the roadside bank and it was a beautiful sunny evening.

My good friend, Robert Hales, with whom I do most of my carp fishing. Rob holds a superb 49lb common.

Ritchie had brought the curry and I had brought the pudding and we were having a nice glass of wine – great days indeed. I remember going to sleep a happy man, and in such a situation it was hard to do anything more but I was awoken at dawn to my buzzer screaming and in autopilot and I lifted the rod into a good fish that fought like a tiger. Five minutes later, Ritchie landed a 38lb 4oz lightly scaled mirror that has since grown to well over forty pounds. This was a fitting end to a great session on a great venue.

Rainbow Lake

My next venue is France and has to be Rainbow Lake. Everyone has heard about Rainbow Lake and no doubt you have all seen photographs of the place, but, believe me, nothing can prepare you for your first sight of this lake. Imagine an area in the ground that goes up and down like the surface of the moon. Now put trees and bushes around everywhere and fill it up with water. Now stock it with a super strain of carp that grow to world record proportions and will probably reach ninety pounds in the next five years and you have Rainbow Lake. It is truly an awesome place and can only be described as a 'full metal jacket' or 'hardcore' water. There is no room for beginners to carp fishing here; indeed, this is a place that can break the heart of even a hardened carper. I remember looking at Dave Treasure's face when he first looked at Peg 21 on Rainbow. Dave has been there and bought the T-shirt on more than a few occasions on all kinds of waters and is a carp angler at the highest level, but his face dropped off when he walked into Peg 21. Mine wasn't a lot better and I'd played near two thousand pounds of great white shark off the Cape of Good Hope – are you now getting the picture? Fallen trees, islands everywhere, branches sticking up from the bottom and it's even worse under the water!

Rainbow Lake in France.

Don't you just love 'em!

This is the kind of lake you either hate and make excuses why you aren't catching, or that you just tackle head on for success. Then when you do succeed on such a water it really means something. Being an all-rounder, it's probable that the week before I set eyes on Rainbow I was roach or dace fishing, just imagine the impact this water had on me. I took it on and learnt how to fish it by taking the advice of the

likes of Bob Davis and Steve Briggs, and now the water has become one of my all-time favourites. I would imagine the fishing was the same before the fish kill at Raduta, for when you sit on Rainbow on your chair and the buzzer sounds off, it could be an 'average' fish of thirty-five pounds. If you are lucky a fifty-pound common, indeed a sixty-pound common, a seventy-pound mirror or even one of the eighty-pound fish that live in the lake! Every time I get a run on Rainbow I think, 'this could be the world record', and that's what keeps me going back.

Woodpecker Pool

My second water in England is 'Wood-pecker Pool', the water where I caught my first thirty-pounder, as mentioned above, a two-acre 'pond' in the Shropshire country-side. It was not a syndicate that fished, just seven mates. Rarely did two people fish it at once; we always phoned to see who was going to be there and when, so we could avoid one other and make sure we always had the lake to ourselves. There was a boathouse with a TV, microwave, cooker and sink and outside the doors was one of the best swims. It was a place to get your head straight and enjoy being on your own. I made a video there and in two days I had a 20lb and 30lb cat. I also caught a 21lb full-scale mirror, a 30lb 4oz leather and a 31lb mirror. Sadly the farmer got married and they didn't want us on the land any more although it was half a mile from the farmhouse. Still, I and all the rest of the lads have memories of a very special place indeed.

River Ebro

Last but not least is my second foreign water, in Spain, where I go fishing with my old Brummie mate, Colin Bunn. Colin runs a great guiding service down in the town of Mequinenza, on the junction of the Ebro and Segre rivers, which has the best winter fishing for carp anywhere in the world. The fish are mainly commons in the twenty- to thirty-pound range, but com-mons over forty pounds are not rare and getting bigger every year – a common over sixty pounds was caught in 2004 and I'm sure there are bigger fish in the River Ebro.

The nice thing about this venue is that in January and February when the worst of the weather is going on in England, you can jump on a plane and be in Spain in two hours. Colin picks you up at the airport, and two hours after that you are looking at the river. Within an hour you can be land-ing your first 20lb or even 40lb common, which is what I call winter fishing!

The other thing I like about this place is that it's a river rather than a lake, which makes it different. Don't get put off; it's not like fishing a shallow, fast-running river where your lead is being swept down-stream all the time. No, it's easy fishing, just different. It's civilized as well for there is no night fishing, and I mean no night fishing – you certainly don't want trouble with a Spanish policeman. You start at dawn and finish at dark, which is usually about 7pm at this time of year. Then it's time for a shower in the apartment and then out for dinner and a little wine or a beer. Now that's carp fishing. It's a special winter venue and worth a visit. I will return many times.

THE FUTURE

Carp fishing has come a long way in a short time. I remember only twenty-five years ago there were no specialist carp magazines, carp gear was in very few shops and most anglers were fishing for roach and perch. The first rod they bought was a 13ft float rod and very few pleasure anglers owned a buzzer or a carp rod. Then something happened which was called the hair-rig, suddenly the catching of carp was made easy, compared to the old rigs. You didn't need to sit over your rods, strike at any movement and then miss 99 per cent of your takes. Now with the hair-rig you waited for the reel handle to go round and reeled them in! They even designed

A Spanish 35lb+ carp.

Snow in Spain proves it's not all sun in that country.

the Shimano Baitrunner so you don't lose your rod on the take, that's how easy it has become.

More and more anglers wanted to catch a decent fish and who could blame them. Kids needed to decide whether they wanted to catch a gudgeon on the canal on a whip or a fifteen-pound carp whilst sleeping in a bedchair listening to garage music. No contest. I remember seeing the first £200 Fox bedchair and wondering who would buy one of those when you could buy one from the supermarket for less than a tenner. However, buy them they did, and companies like Fox, Nash and Shimano turn over millions of pounds all over the world. Carp fishing has become big business and is growing by the second. I know! I have a bait company and it's hard to keep up with at times.

What of the future? I think it will be more of the same, with even the USA going carp mad; believe me, it's already happening. When the Americans take it on,

187

they will buy as much carp gear as the rest of the world put together. I think carp matches – and by that I mean big carp matches spread over one week – will get bigger and bigger; indeed, on the continent they are already a major part of carp fishing. We think we are serious in our carp fishing, but carp anglers in the likes of Slovakia, Czech Republic, Romania and Hungary are absolutely fanatical about the sport and fish matches every other week for big money. America has already jumped on the bandwagon and have contests where you can win $25,000 and a car. Already our big carpers, like Tim Paisley, Steve Briggs, Simon Crow and John Lilley are jumping on planes to travel to fish competitions, and these matches will be on the increase over the next five years. Who would have thought it twenty-five years ago: a lake as big as an inland sea in Europe filled to the brim with carp anglers fishing for big money?

I think tackle will continue to move on too. Let's face it, companies have to change so they can make more sales. I see more bait boats coming, and boilie guns run by compressed air that fire boilies or even rigs as far as you like. Soon there will be marker floats with a lead that has a camera fitted so you can see what's going on in the swims, so you will be able to sit there in your swim and see the fish take the bait. GPS systems will come into play so when you find a hot spot on a lake you can go back there the next time you visit the venue. I can even see the staple bivvy being old hat, with fisheries having special 'sheds' on the swims, complete with electricity, running water and a bed. I know one company has already brought out a special trailer bivvy which you take to the lake on the back of the car – pop it up and it's home from home and specially designed for carp anglers.

However, with all this growth comes the pressure of anglers wanting more venues and more big fish. Luckily a lot of the match venues that were stocked years ago with $\frac{1}{2}$lb–2lb fish are now full of 10–20lb fish. All those fisheries can either change over to being a specimen carp water or simply sell them to the carp waters and use some of the proceeds to start off again with $\frac{1}{2}$lb–2lb fish. But there are still not enough carp, and we will see more fish coming from abroad. There is even talk of carp from as far away as Australia as big as 100lb – can you imagine that one on your 2lb TC carp rod? These fish bring new problems and especially disease and new viruses. No matter what I say they will come to these shores and there will be anglers queuing up to fish for them, even the anglers that have opposed them in the first place will find it hard to say no to the chance to catch a 100lb carp.

We must prepare for this and new rules should be made, the main one being that no one can carry a landing net, unhooking mat or weigh sling from one water to another; in other words, every water supplies these products. That way the risk of disease being spread can be cut by probably 99 per cent. A modern-day carp angler could be fishing a water in Devon one day and then be fishing a water in Scotland two days later. One week later, he could be fishing a contest in France and then back to Birmingham. You can see the problems this could cause so it's best to prepare in advance.

The future is rosy for carp fishing as long as we look after the sport and start putting plans into place now. I will continue to enjoy my trout fishing, sea fishing and dace fishing, but I will always return to sitting behind a couple of carp rods waiting for the buzzer to sound. It's a great sport and I have so much to thank carp fishing for. Long may that continue.

Appendix

Top 20 UK Carp (as of September 2006)
By Chris Ball

Weight	Captured	Fish name	Venue	Captor
65lb 14oz	October 2005	Two-Tone	Conningbrook	Simon Bater
65lb 8oz	September 2005	Two-Tone	Conningbrook	Dan Markwick
64lb 10oz	June 2006	Two-Tone	Conningbrook	Dave Milne
64lb 5oz	February 2005	Two-Tone	Conningbrook	Jon Pack
64lb 5oz	July 2006	Two-Tone	Conningbrook	Jon McAllister
63lb 8oz	June 2004	Two-Tone	Conningbrook	Paul Dedman
63lb	June 2006	Two-Tone	Conningbrook	Keith Gilbert
62lb 6oz	July 2006	Two-Tone	Conningbrook	Jim Hepper
62lb	April 2004	Two-Tone	Conningbrook	Steve Allcott
61lb 7oz	August 2002	Two-Tone	Conningbrook	Lee Jackson
61lb 4oz	July 2006	–	Essex Stillwater	Mark Holmes
61lb	October 2001	Two-Tone	Conningbrook	Gary Bayes
61lb	June 2003	Two-Tone	Conningbrook	Jim Shelley
61lb	October 2004	–	Ringstead	Roy Jackson
60lb 12oz	May 2003	Benson	Bluebell	David Waby
60lb 9oz	August 2002	Two-Tone	Conningbrook	Brett White
60lb 8oz	June 2003	Benson	Bluebell	Kyle Smith
60lb 2oz	April 2003	Benson	Bluebell	Andy Childs
60lb 1oz	May 2004	Benson	Bluebell	Mark Brisley
60lb	May 2003	The Lady	Ringstead	Tony Maule

As can be seen, to get into the top twenty list of carp caught in this country you need to bank, unbelievably, a carp of more than sixty pounds! This shows just how carp weights have escalated in recent years. Though the list shows the dominance of Two-Tone (this carp has headed the list five times in the last six years) there are a number of other different carp that have topped 55lb+ in recent times. Some of these will no doubt better 60lb in the near future.

One fish that stands out from the rest is the 61lb 4oz mirror captured by Mark Holmes, as it fell to a surface bait. Who would have ever thought that a 60lb+ floater-caught carp would be banked in this country? Quite amazing.

Index